envision:
a handbook

supporting young people's participation in galleries and the arts

Written by
Jo Wheeler and Amber Walls,
with Steve Little and Francois Matarasso

Editor
Eileen Daly

Proofing
Jack Fortescue

Designers
SteersMcGillan Design Ltd

Printer
Short Run Press

Published July 2008 by
engage, Suite AG, City Cloisters,
196 Old Street, London EC1V 9FR

Further copies available from
www.engage.org/publications

engage is a registered company limited
by guarantee in England and Wales
no. 4194208. Registered charity no.1087471

ISBN 978-0-9559088-2-8

engage is committed to maximising
access throughout its programmes.
This publication is available in a range of
formats. For more information, contact
info@engage.org

engage is the leading international membership
association for gallery education working with
arts and education professionals. engage has
over 1,000 members including gallery
educators, teachers and arts professionals
from across the UK and in 15 countries.
engage's work helps galleries encourage
people to participate in and enjoy the visual
arts and become confident users of galleries
and museums.

envision supports galleries in England to
engage with young people, sharing ideas,
expertise, resources, and creating
opportunities for young people to have a
genuine role in shaping gallery practice, policy
and spaces. envision is managed by engage
and was funded by the Department for
Communities and Local Government and
Arts Council England Grants for the Arts,
with support from the Calouste Gulbenkian
Foundation, the Yorkshire Building Society
Charitable Trust and the Rayne Foundation.

Disclaimer
All text has been published to present useful
information and to stimulate thinking and
generate debate and ideas. engage does not
guarantee the accuracy of the information
contained within the writing and all opinions
expressed are those of the contributors.

Cover image: Metropole Gallery, LivingART project 2007

Contents

Articles

'LivingArt', Metropole Gallery, Tool Wall, 2006

Jane Sillis

engage is the lead organisation for gallery education in the UK and internationally, promoting access to and enjoyment of the visual arts. engage works in four key areas:

• research and projects
• sharing practice
• advocacy
• continuing professional development

Our 1100 members in 15 countries include gallery professionals, artists, teachers, and youth workers. engage reaches millions of gallery visitors each year through our programmes and through our members' work.

For the last five years envision has been a key aspect of engage's work, supporting galleries to embrace youth friendly practice. Thirty-two galleries have participated in envision across England. Most recently the programme in Yorkshire, South East, South West and Eastern Region has been supported by the Department for Communities and Local Government, Arts Council England, the Rayne Foundation and the Calouste Gulbenkian Foundation.

envision connects with policies and initiatives for young people and the arts, such as Every Child Matters, Find Your Talent – the government's commitment to a cultural offer for young people, and the new Creative Apprenticeships. This publication offers sound advice from a broad range of professionals who have engaged on equal terms with young people on arts projects. It is a privilege to have access to practical advice from colleagues who enjoy and understand the value of working in partnership with young people.

Thanks to Jo Wheeler and Amber Walls who have co-ordinated envision and the young people, artists, educators, galleries and others involved in the delivery of envision and to the envision advisory group.

3

Introduction

This guide is packed with:

- Advice and comments from lots of different experts

- Good practice examples, top tips and jargon busters

- Information about current policy legislation and the big agendas affecting working with young people

- Signposts to further help and resources

- Inspiration and ideas

This handbook is a practical guide to involving young people in galleries.

It is designed to be a useful resource providing you with the advice, information and inspiration you need to get started, refresh your knowledge or to improve what you are already doing. It can be dipped into, customised with your own notes and generally used rather than left to gather dust.

The positive contribution of the arts to young people's lives has been widely documented. The announcement in early 2008 that the government is committed to creating a cultural offer for all young people aged 0–19 years old in the UK (at least five hours a week of cultural activity in and out of school) acknowledges this and puts culture firmly on the map. The government's paper on the cultural offer clearly identifies that galleries should be an essential part of the offer.

Over the last decade galleries have begun to successfully reach out to young people, demonstrating a whole host of ways in which they can genuinely involve and benefit young people. This has led to an ongoing debate in some circles questioning whether the arts have become too much of a government 'tool'. If you aren't already convinced by the role of galleries in achieving genuine social outcomes you should be by the time you get to the end of this book, which is full of examples, persuasive arguments and countless good reasons why we should all want to involve young people in galleries. If you are convinced but you need practical advice or help to convince others around you, read on.

This publication has grown out of envision, engage's national action research programme championing a youth-friendly culture in galleries. Through research, projects, networking, advocacy and professional development, envision has supported galleries to engage with young people, helping to build skills and confidence in galleries and young people working together.

The wealth of envision learning and inspiration is encapsulated in this handbook and focuses on young people aged 14–21 years old outside of formal mainstream education, but the content is relevant to working with all young people. Drawing examples from across the sector it offers expert advice from respected professionals across a wide range of relevant fields.

We would like to thank all the galleries and young people who have supported and contributed to envision over the years, whose vision and commitment has shaped this book.

A big thank you goes to the following colleagues for their advice and contributions:

Richard Beales, Outreach and Inclusions Manager, Towner Art Gallery

Trish Evans, Creative Room Manager, Nottingham Children's Services

Johnny Gailey, Opt in for Art Co-ordinator, Fruitmarket Gallery

Virginia Howarth Galt, Director, Artswork

Cath Hawes, Senior Arts Development Manager, Shape

Penny Jones, Watch this Space Co-ordinator

Barbara Taylor, Programme Director, enquire

Clare Mitchell, Regional Youth Officer, Government Office West Midlands

Chris Naylor, Cultural Regeneration, Culture, Policy and Management, City University

Simon Richey, Director of Education, Gulbenkian Foundation

Dr Veronica Sekules, Head of Education and Research, Sainsbury Centre for Visual Arts

Rachel Tranter, Head of Arts, Richmond Borough Council at Orleans House Gallery

Dr Jacqueline Watson, Visiting Fellow, Centre for Applied Research in Education, University of East Anglia

And a special thank you for his contribution to 'The big ideas' to:

Harry Wade, Development Officer, Participation Works, National Youth Agency

[1] See *Crossing the Line: Extending Young People's Access to Cultural Venues*, John Harland and Kay Kinder (eds), Calouste Gulbenkian Foundation, 1999, and *Funky on Your Flyer*, Richard Ings, Arts Council England, 2001. engage's national conference Young People 16:25> ART in 2001 corroborated the research report findings.

envision: a two-way dialogue

The envision programme supports galleries to work with young people to develop youth-friendly practice and policy.

The term youth-friendly practice and policy was coined to reflect the idea that to successfully involve young people in galleries we need to embrace a youth-friendly ethos at the heart of our institutions and to consider how we achieve this across programming, front of house, marketing and staffing, and not just in our education work.

A funky education event may do wonders to excite young participants, but if they decide to come back with their friends, the memory of a great time won't be enough if every other aspect of the venue is designed around adult visitors with specialist art knowledge.

In 2001 engage research[1] highlighted that:

• Young people were progressively losing interest in arts venues in their teens
• Opportunities for young people were very limited
• Cultural venues had big gaps in youth expertise

There was a strong message that to involve young people in cultural venues we had to acknowledged them as real stakeholders – that they have something valuable to offer us, and that we should embrace young people's own interpretation of culture.

Through the envision programme engage has supported over 32 galleries, arts and youth organisations of all shapes and sizes across England. Together we explored how organisations working in very different situations could genuinely embrace young people and place them at the heart of their thinking.

The projects were designed to create a dialogue with young people through a range of creative consultation and research projects. This helped the venues develop new skills, policy and practice which was genuinely informed by young people's own culture, ideas and experiences.

In many instances the projects have led to new ways of involving young people in a range of mutually beneficial roles: as organisational decision-makers and advisers, guides, peer educators and mentors, ambassadors and advocates, volunteers, trainees, trainers, staff and as co-programmers developing lively and sustainable creative programmes for their peers.

Highlights from these projects are used to illustrate the different sections of this handbook, and full case study reports are available on the envision website www.en-vision.org.uk

> **❝** We used the term 'cultural hybrid' in Crossing the Line to describe an approach based on mutual recognition and respect, where cultural venues go out to young people to discuss programming and where young people are encouraged to go to cultural venues. We are arguing for two-way traffic. A two-way culture.**❞**
>
> *Simon Richey, Director of Education, Calouste Gulbenkian Foundation*

The big ideas

I think that you should put posters up around school

Need more Deco
on the upstirs and
Down Stires

Background
music while your here

Amber Walls

Why involve young people in galleries? For most organisations there are three main reasons:

You know you want to
Galleries have an enormous amount to offer young people and young people have an enormous amount to offer galleries.

You know you have to
Young people have the right to access cultural provision, and in the current social and political climate galleries, alongside other public institutions, are expected to demonstrate their public benefit.

You know you can't afford to miss out
Unless you are happy to miss out on a multitude of new opportunities, key funding sources and exciting new developments in galleries.

This section gives you a potted history of issues and opportunities affecting work with young people in galleries. It identifies why they are relevant to you and how you can make the most of them.

You know you want to

Because galleries have a huge and at times unique contribution to offer young people

Galleries are in a position to use the arts as an effective tool for engaging young people, offering spaces and resources to create fantastic learning opportunities.

"Phenomenal. So many doors opened. Never had such a great and free opportunity. One big exciting roller coaster where you don't know where the next turn is coming – up and down."

Young participant, envision project, Nottingham Castle Museum and Art Gallery

Because young people have a huge and unique contribution to offer galleries

Young people can help make our organisations relevant and fresh.

"Our new youth-friendly space that young people helped us to create turned out to be people-friendly. The visitors loved it."

Gallery educator, Manchester Art Gallery

Because we're all concerned about the well-being of our young population

We know that galleries can play a valuable role in the lives of vulnerable and disadvantaged young people. National concern about young people's well-being appears to be growing, with daily negative news reports and bleak statistics about levels of school exclusion, educational under-achievement, teenage pregnancy, drug and alcohol use, the increasing fear of youth crime and the emergence of ASBOS and hoodies. A recent report put the UK at the bottom of a league table of child well-being across 21 industrialised nations.[1]

"We are turning out a generation of young people who are unhappy, unhealthy, engaging in risky behaviour, who have poor relationships with their families and peers, have low expectations and don't feel safe."

Sir Al Aynsley-Green, Children's Commissioner for England

KickstART, Thelma Hubert Gallery, 2007

Because you want to be at the forefront of current and exciting developments in galleries

As a gallery educator you can get directly involved in working with young people and new partners to address these issues and champion the role of culture and community in society.

"Education in galleries is a very distinctive practice, benefiting from the professional involvement of artists as teachers, collaborators, activists and mentors. This has given gallery education a real edge and experimental quality. The work of education departments is the main route through which many young people are attracted to becoming involved in galleries as audiences and practitioners. Through international contacts, collaborations and partnerships, many of them initiated by the independent gallery education agency, engage, it is clear that practice in the UK is leading the world."

Turning Point: A Strategy for the Contemporary Visual Arts, Arts Council England, 2006

There are many examples from envision and elsewhere of the special contribution galleries can make to the development, learning and inclusion of young people experiencing challenges in their lives. National interest in the role of the arts in tackling social problems has grown significantly over the last decade and in recent years the arts have become a central feature of policies and initiatives designed to tackle issues faced by vulnerable and disadvantaged young people. Some of these initiatives include: Creative Partnerships, Positive Activities for Young People and the Youth Justice Board/ Arts Council England initiative to deliver creative learning opportunities for young people at risk of offending.

[1] *Child Poverty in Perspective: An Overview of Child Well-being in Rich Countries*, UNICEF Report Card 7, UNICEF Innocenti Research Centre, Florence, 2007

Galleries can offer young people opportunities to

- Acquire practical creative skills and discover talent
- Access unique resources
- Contribute to personal development using the arts as a tool to build self-confidence, empower young people and re-engage with learning
- Achieve and gain accreditation – a chance to have a positive relationship with learning
- Build a positive self-perception to confirm that they are a valued group of individuals, who have something positive to contribute to society
- Engage in a positive learning experience and be able to lead the direction of their learning
- Develop positive relationships with adults, ie, gallery staff, artists and support staff
- Access to high profile spaces to showcase and value their work
- Have somewhere to go – a new social opportunity particularly for marginalised and isolated young people

Young people can offer galleries opportunities to

- Develop a two-way relationship with young people, to break down barriers and stereotypes on both sides
- Develop the reputation and profile of the gallery within the local community and beyond
- Fulfill a public duty – many galleries rely increasingly on public funds and galleries have a responsibility to the public to use their resources to contribute to social inclusion, citizenship and young people's learning and development
- Provide a positive and valued contribution to galleries' collections, interpretation, curation and displays by adding contemporary experiences, opinions and material
- Increase and broaden audiences through their friends, family and other networks
- Broaden diversity of the gallery workforce – young people are the potential future employees of the gallery and will bring diversity in culture and background, reflecting the local community
- Keep galleries forward thinking and dynamic by enabling them to engage with the next generation

" UK is accused of failing children as it comes bottom of a league table for child well-being across 21 industrialised countries. "

BBC News 24, 14 February 2007

> **"** When I first saw this young man he wore a hooded jacket with hood up and peaked cap with the peak pulled down over his eyes. However when he was showing people around his exhibition he wore no jacket or hat, just a proud expression on his face. **"**
>
> *Staff member of Pupil Referral Unit following the Game On project at Qube Gallery, Oswestry*

'Game On', Cube, 2004

You know you have to

Because young people have a right to access public cultural provision

Young people's right to access cultural and artistic opportunities is enshrined in Article 31 of the United Nations Convention on the Rights of the Child (UNCRC) 1989.

" Parties shall respect and promote the right of the child to participate fully in cultural and artistic life and shall encourage the provision of appropriate and equal opportunities for cultural, artistic, recreational and leisure activity. **"**

UNCRC, 1989

Because as public venues we have a responsibility to ensure equality of access to our services

It is no secret that young people, outside of school, college or university visits, are unlikely to be independant visitors to galleries, which don't figure highly on the list of cool things to do for an average teenager. Research tells us that the problem isn't young people's disinterest in the arts, but the fact that arts venues don't cater for young people. In fact some would say that we are actively excluding young people.

" Young people between the ages of 14 and 18, research suggests, are often disinclined to visit cultural venues such as theatres, concert halls, galleries and museums. It is possible for a young person to experience only a fleeting acquaintance with venues of this kind and to cease to visit them, not necessarily because they dislike a particular artform but because these venues do not appear to offer what is relevant to them. **"**

Extending Young People's Access to Cultural Venues, Arts Council England and Calouste Gulbenkian Foundation, 1999

Because the social and political climate has put galleries under new pressure to contribute to key policy agendas

Government policy and thinking always has a direct impact on the work that we do at a local level. Whether you are interested in politics or not, it is important to be aware of the national picture and of the main interests of government. It will help you to make sense of – and possibly predict – new policies, strategies and opportunities which will directly affect your work. It will also help you to speak the right language to persuade, influence and communicate effectively, whether this is with funding bodies, managers or partners.

Over the last decade, government thinking has had a dramatic affect on work in the arts and galleries. There has been a lot of interest in the value of the arts to society and specifically in the value of the arts and creativity in improving educational attainment, health and well-being and in tackling social inequalities and helping to promote social inclusion.

For galleries, social inclusion isn't just about increasing access to our venues, it is about the role of galleries in contributing to wider social outcomes such as attainment, health and crime reduction.

Alongside other cultural institutions, galleries have traditionally been seen as an activity that is enjoyed and valued by a 'specialist' audience rather than by the masses. The last decade has seen an enormous drive to make galleries accessible and relevant to broader communities. Funding for the arts has become more focused on public benefit rather than just on artistic excellence. Education and access have become an increasingly important function and the role of galleries in delivering wider social and economic benefits has increased.

In the last few years access, education and 'socially engaged' arts programmes have flourished across galleries. Partnerships have developed between galleries and homeless networks, drug and advice agencies, alternative education providers, neighbourhood regeneration projects, health and youth justice networks.

New flagship galleries such as Tate Modern, The New Art Gallery Walsall, Baltic in Gateshead, the Lowry Centre in Salford, Turner Contemporary in Margate and Fact in Liverpool, have been central features of urban regeneration projects and have prioritised involvement with local residents and communities.

Because we are required to provide evidence to demonstrate our public benefit

Like all public services, galleries have increasingly been required to be accountable. Evaluation and reporting have become basic requirements of gallery education and today much of our funding depends on our ability to produce credible evidence and to articulate the value of our work to the public.

Because we need to demonstrate that we are actively involving the public in making decisions about our services

Active participation is about involving the public in making decisions about services we offer. The last decade has seen active participation grow in strength from an ideal, to a government policy commitment, to a requirement attached to much of the funding available for cultural provision, to a statutory requirement of new policy and practice governing work with young people, including Every Child Matters and Youth Matters.[2]

So if you are working with people, you need to demonstrate how you are actively involving them in shaping and influencing your provision.

[2] *Every Child Matters: Change for Children* is a government policy, which was introduced in 2004. Youth Matters focuses on the government's vision for work with young people aged 13–19 years old.

"They can have sex when they're 16, they can vote when they're 18, but they have to become middle class and middle-aged before they can engage with art? So we should do it. And we MUST do it too because we all want a world with art and culture in it. We want good design and good cooking and good writing and good films and good business. We want all the things that come from creative people, people who know about art, about thinking about or making art. And we know that being involved with art makes people better communicators, more tolerant – essential today as well. So we must do it."

Chris Naylor, Director, Cultural Regeneration, Culture, Policy & Management, City University

Bow Arts Trust worked with local young people to design a new arts building as part of Leaside Generation's public consultation for the Bow area

Galleries have demonstrated that consultation with young people through visual arts activities is engaging, fun and an effective way of gaining opinions about gallery provision and wider local agendas such as Children's Services and local regeneration plans.

Because galleries need young people to be interested – to be the consumers, participants and creative leaders of the future

We must engage young people to secure the future of our galleries and creative culture. If we exclude them now why should we expect them to be interested as adults?

"I'm writing this on 20 November 2007: the 18th birthday of the United Nations Convention on the Rights of the Child. All children and young people have a right to protection and certain provision and they also have participation rights. Article 12 of the UNCRC states that young people have the right to have a say in all matters that affect them and for their views to be taken seriously. But apart from the rights angle, it's just common sense to include a big group of people who don't use galleries that much, by asking them how to make your gallery more attractive to them. It's the sound of innovation, the shape of things to come… you just have to listen!"

Harry Wade, Development Officer, Participation Works, the National Youth Agency

ODIvision, Our East End', Bow Arts Trust, 2006

Because we need to create a more diverse workforce in galleries

Building relationships with young people from a wide range of backgrounds is one important way of working towards this.

It's no secret that galleries are populated by a predominantly white, female, middle class workforce and we would all like to change this. Working with young people can bring in fresh new perspectives, ideas and definitions of culture in the short-term. In the long-term it may help to make our workforce more diverse and more representational of society as a whole.

The workforce in visual arts is highly educated: 47% with a first degree and a further 40% with a post-graduate degree or diploma. 93% of the visual arts workforce is white and 75% is female.

" The representation of black and minority ethnic groups in visual arts organisations is low at 5%. There are few black or Asian middle-level curators. This reflects the widespread use of staff recruited through exclusive social networks. **"**

Turning Point: A Strategy for the Contemporary Visual Arts, Arts Council England, 2006

Because we can offer young people pathways into exciting future interests and career opportunities

Don't forget that the cultural and creative sector is one of the fastest growing industries in the UK and is increasingly important to our economic future as a country. Creative and cultural industries account for 7.3% of all UK economic activity, contributing £60 billion to the economy.

" In the North East, investment in major new cultural institutions such as Baltic and Sage – both in Gateshead – has been the catalyst for the £1 billion redevelopment of East Gateshead, leading to the creation of 10,000 jobs, plus a further 40 full-time jobs servicing the gallery's catering and bar functions. **"**

Turning Point: A Strategy for the Contemporary Visual Arts, Arts Council England, 2006

Because people want to be involved in galleries

Did you know that public interest in the arts and in galleries is at an all time high?
- 79% of the public agree that arts and cultural projects should receive public funding
- More people take part in cultural activity than vote
- 7 of the top 10 visitor attractions in the UK are publicly funded museums and galleries
- 82% of British people want to have a museum or art gallery in their local town
- Since the opening of Baltic, residents are 40% more in favour of centres for contemporary art than they were before, and over 80% believe that interest in arts and culture has increased since the gallery opened[3]

[3] All figures are from *Values and Vision: The Contribution of Culture*, Arts Council England, Museums, Libraries and Archives Council and National Museum Directors Conference, 2006

'Generator' · ArtSway Gallery, 2007

A very potted history of political interest in young people and culture

1960s

Community arts movement champions the value of arts and culture to social well-being.

1980s

Conservative government begins to establish access and community based arts initiatives including the arts in urban regeneration projects and began changing the focus of National Lottery funding away from large prestigious capital projects to community initiatives.

1997

New Labour elected to power. Interest in arts participation increased, with a special interest in the transformative nature of creativity. Former prime minister Tony Blair is reported to have said in 1997: 'I will tell you why Labour wants to put arts on the agenda, because the Labour Party believes that art and culture enrich the quality of our life. Because developing the potential of every individual is an essential part of our creed... Our future depends on our creativity.'[4]

1998

New Labour sets up the Social Exclusion Unit (SEU). SEU worked with government departments to commission research reports investigating the role of different provision in tackling poverty and exclusion. The PAT 10 Research Report: Arts and Neighbourhood Renewal, concluded that: 'arts... cultural and recreational activity can contribute to neighbourhood renewal and make a real difference to health, crime, employment and education in deprived communities'.

2001

Government invests £100 million in Renaissance in the Regions, a programme 'bringing new life to regional museums, libraries, archives and galleries'. Through its audience development and education programmes, Renaissance in the Regions has fully embraced a role in helping to address social inclusion stating that: 'museums and galleries have an important part to play in education, learning, access, social inclusion, neighbourhood renewal, the regions, and the modernisation of public services.'[5]

2002

Creative Partnerships is set up with huge government investment to work with schools in 16 of the most deprived areas of England using creativity to raise aspirations and achievements across the schools curriculum.

2006

'places to go and things to do' comes top of the list of things young people in Britain say they want (Youth Matters). It becomes the mantra for the government's policy priorities for young people.

2007

Aiming High: Positive Activities for Young People – the government's 10-year strategy for youth work sets out a vision for providing positive activities, including cultural participation.

2008

Government announces the intention to develop five hours a week cultural offer to all young people aged between 0–19 years old. Find Your Talent pilot schemes scheduled to begin 2008/09. Creative Partnerships is rolled out nationally.

You know you you can't afford to miss out

Young people, social inclusion and participation are high on national and political agendas and there are many new strategies, policies and related resources that can bring you a host of new opportunities.

Here are three key developments and policies to help you stay on top of the national scene that will affect your work at a local level.

The cultural offer/ Find Your Talent

The cultural offer sets out the government's commitment to providing a basic entitlement to cultural activity for all young people aged 0–19 years old, with an emphasis on school age. It aims to ensure that all children and young people have the chance to participate in at least five hours of high quality culture a week in and out of school. This involves:

• Learning in and about culture – helping young people to develop as informed and reflective spectators, participants and creators
• Learning through culture – using participation in culture to boost creativity, attainment and personal development

The offer is expected to include a range of activities including seeing and taking part in activities at galleries, museums, heritage sites, library and archive services, theatre, music and dance performances, learning a musical instrument, filmmaking, creative writing and producing visual arts or crafts.

Ten Find Your Talent pilot projects started in 2008. The cultural offer clearly acknowledges acceptance of the value of cultural participation for young people, both as a valuable experience in itself and as a means to support young people's personal and life skills.

What you could do

See www.creative-partnerships.com for more information. Alternatively you could contact your local Creative Partnerships office or Arts Council England education department to find out about local activty, contacts and opportunities.

Every Child Matters and Youth Matters

Every Child Matters: Change for Children was introduced in 2004 and is the government policy at the heart of all work with young people from 0–19 years old in England and Wales. If you are working with children and young people you need to know about it. Every Child Matters came about as a result of the Victoria Climbie enqiry, a highly critical report into the death of eight-year-old Victoria Climbie in 2000 who was tortured by her relatives and whose death highlighted the failure of the public services to protect her.

Every Child Matters aims to ensure that all children and young people regardless of background or circumstance should have the support they need to achieve the five Every Child Matters outcomes: stay safe, be healthy, enjoy and achieve, make a positive contribution and achieve economic well-being.

Things you should know about Every Child Matters:

- The five outcomes are at the centre of all work with children and young people carried out at a local and national level. For the first time all local agencies are working towards the same outcomes
- Each local authority will have a single Children and Young People's Plan shared across all local government, voluntary and community sector providers which clearly sets out area priorities developed in collaboration with local people
- As part of Every Child Matters a Children's Trust has been set up in every local authority area with responsibility for integrated planning, commissioning and delivery of local services overseen by a Strategic Children and Young People's Board. If you are seeking funding for work with children and young people locally you should find out more about commissioning
- It is now a statutory requirement that children and young people have a say about provision which affects them, meaning that you need to incorporate this into your work with young people if you have public funding

What you could do

See www.everychildmatters.gov.uk for more information. The website has a useful outcomes framework chart taking you through all the statutory national outcomes that organisations working with children and young people will be working towards. It will help you to recognise at a glance what you can contribute to.

Check out *Art Matters*, the Arts Council England, North East publication demonstrating how the arts can deliver Every Child Matters. See www.artscouncil.org.uk/documents/ for more details.

Get in touch with your local Children's Trust or the person responsible for leading on the Children and Young People's Plan in your local authority to find out how your work can contribute to the local plan or to access funding through your local commissioning process.

Youth Matters builds on Every Child Matters and adopts the same five guiding outcomes for young people aged 13–19 years old. *Youth Matters: Next Steps* sets out the government's vision for work with young people and is based on national consultation with young people which identified that they want: 'somewhere to go, something to do and someone to talk to'.

Youth Matters emphasises young people having more choice and influence over services and facilities that are available to them. It also encourages volunteering and local community engagement.

Youth Matters: Next Steps forms part of the wider government youth offer that includes better support for families, more youth-friendly accessible health services and greater access to sports, culture and the arts.

Order your copy of *Youth Matters: Next Steps*. See www.everychildmatters.gov.uk for more information.

14–19 Educational Reform

This aims to transform learning for 14–19 year olds. The reforms are designed to provide a more flexible range of learning routes suited to the diverse needs of learners and to the needs of employers. It also aims to encourage more young people to stay in post-16 learning.

A key development for galleries is vocational learning. Every 14–19 year old will be able to choose from 14 different diplomas in addition to the existing National Curriculum. This includes the Creative and Media Diploma currently being piloted and due to be rolled out nationwide from September 2008. Combining practical experience of working in industry with traditional functional skills, for example English, maths and ICT, the diplomas will be delivered through collaboration between different educational institutions (schools and colleges) and creative and media organisations and industries. Employers from the cultural sector, including museums and galleries, are being asked to support and develop these new initiatives.

What you could do

See www.dfes.gov.uk/14–19 or www.skillset.org/qualifications/diploma

See Resources for more information on current policy and initiatives.

'Creative Consultants'
Manchester Art Gallery, 2004

Getting started

I think there
should be more
3-D pictures
Like this
because there

**Jo Wheeler, Steve Little
and Francois Matarasso**

So you want to bring young people into your organisation – you have the personal enthusiasm to work with a new and exciting group of people and want to bring life into your organisation – but before you dive in you'll need to ask yourself some specific questions about the kind of project you want to run.

What would suit the specific circumstances of your gallery – your location, size, skills, collection and resources?

What is the local need for your project?

Who do you want to work with?

This section will help you to answer those questions and in particular looks at ways of pulling together the partnerships, resources, ideas and the essential planning required to inform your work with young people.

Partnership Working

Partnership working not only makes good sense but is arguably an absolute necessity in today's working world. So what are the benefits of partnership working? What makes a good partner? Why do they fail? How do you go about forming one?

10 benefits of partnership working

- Ability to share resources
- Extra capacity
- Different perspectives
- Increased networks
- Momentum
- Ability to be more strategic – by joining different initiatives and taking up opportunities – not duplicating work
- Spread risk
- Access to a broader range of knowledge, skills and experience
- Sharing effective practice and innovative ideas
- Increased opportunities for training and professional development

10 characteristics of a good partner

- Honest and open about their own reasons for being involved
- Trusting and trustworthy
- Communicates well and listens to others
- Open to different ideas and approaches
- Respects other partners
- Retains focus but is flexible
- Takes on responsibilities and acts on them
- Has a proactive 'can do' approach
- Has integrity
- Wants the partnership to work

10 reasons why partnerships don't work

- Competition between organisations or individuals
- Lack of clarity of purpose or differing perspectives
- Loss of focus
- Poor communication
- The effort spent developing the partnership outstrips the benefits
- Lack of honesty
- Lack of equity – some partners not pulling their weight
- A culture clash between organisations or personality differences
- A lack of flexibility and unwillingness to compromise
- Fear of the unknown and risk-taking

You and your partnerships

As a starting point try carrying out an analysis of the partnerships you are currently involved in or partnerships that exist within your organisation that are relevant to you and your work. By understanding the nature of partnerships you can make them more productive.

Think of a particular partnership and ask yourself the following questions using the lists above as a guide:

Who is involved in the partnership?

Why was the partnership formed and what are its characteristics?

What outcomes does the partnership achieve that would not be achieved if the partnership did not exist?

What do you (or your organisation) give to the partnership and what do you get back?

How could the partnership be improved?

Creating partnerships

Successful partnerships are based on mutual benefit. The benefit does not necessarily have to be equal amongst partners as long as each partner feels that they are getting enough out of it in exchange for their input. If you are involved in a partnership and there is nothing in it for you or your effort far outstrips the gain, question why you are involved. Likewise if you are working with a partner and there is no clear benefit for them don't be surprised if they back off!

Now focus on partnerships that you would like to have and how you might go about developing them. Remember, there is no simple formula to partnership development but the following guidance will provide a useful starting point.

What do you want to achieve? This might be quite general, such as, 'to be more youth-friendly' or more specific as in 'to develop work with disabled young people'. Do you have a specific aim or project you would like to develop or are you more interested in making connections and exploring possibilities?

What do you want from potential partners? Do you have something specific in mind such as advice and support on working with young people, funding, access to networks or to particular groups of young people? Do you want partners from a particular sector: health, education, youth work, youth offending or from a particular geographic area? What sort of partnership are you after? You might find it useful to revisit the earlier section about different types of partnerships to help your thinking.

What can you offer? When considering your potential offer to partners think about the facilities your organisation has and the particular expertise you and your colleagues possess. Your offer might be: a unique collection, visual arts expertise, a free and accessible public space, a neutral community space, a high profile space to exhibit alongside culturally valued arts, the opportunity to give value to young people's creativity and status within their community, the chance to work with positive and neutral role models working in the creative industries, opportunities for creative expression, an alternative informal education space, finance, training, advice or resources for youth staff.

Who to approach

Now that you have an idea of what you want to achieve, who you want to work with and what you can offer, the next step is to find out who might be interested in working with you.

A good starting point is to contact the arts development team at your local or district authority and your regional Arts Council office. They should have a good idea of existing partnership forums, what work is currently happening in your area and advice on who to approach.

You could also contact the Integrated Children's Service at your local authority. Recent changes in the way children's services in England work mean that services formerly provided for children and young people through education, health, youth services and youth offending teams are now integrated into one service. This makes partnership working easier. Your local authority may also have a young people's participation worker and a youth forum.

Other arts and cultural organisations in your area may be interested in exploring how you might work together or they might be involved in partnership forums or have partnerships they want you to be involved in.

You could also try approaching a nearby school or youth club and find out what is happening on a more local level and what interest they might have in working with you. They will be involved in wider partnerships that may be appropriate for you to join.

Young people as partners

Although your partnership might initially be with an organisation, as you involve young people in your organisation and build relationships – perhaps forming a youth panel or advisory group – then your partnership will be with young people. This needs to have the same investment and considerations as any other partnership.

Partnership agreements

Partnerships are driven by people. There is nothing more frustrating than spending years building a relationship with someone from another organisation only to find that they leave and you are back to square one. Be aware of the pitfalls of partnerships that are purely person-led and realise when it can beneficial to formalise a partnership into an organisational agreement.

Partnerships agreements are a useful way of formalising relationships and setting parameters which can be revisited as the relationship progresses to be used as a point of reference if people move on. They are also a means of keeping to the task involved and for resolving areas of conflict.

A partnership agreement might involve:

- an initial meeting to clearly and honestly talk through each partner's agenda
- aim and objectives for the project
- responsibilities
- methods of communication during the project
- evaluation
- documentation, staff involved, skills and training gaps, financial contributions, who's going to manage the budget, support for young people during the project,
- opportunities and support for the young people after the project and future aspirations for the partnership.

It is a good idea to use a written agreement that all partners sign up to, so that everyone is clear about the details of the relationship.

Skill sharing days

Skill sharing days can be a great way of exploring and developing a partnership, but do involve a lot of commitment from both organisations and may be something that neither of you are prepared to commit to until managers are convinced by the investment. Skill sharing sessions can involve staff teams from both organisations and/or young people, to create a joint training opportunity for all to learn from the experience and the expertise of others.

Case study:

Skill sharing

The Castle Museum and Art Gallery in Nottingham held a skill sharing day with City Arts and the Children and Adolescent's Mental Health Services (CAMHs) to help develop a recent partnership between the organisations. The gallery hosted the first section of the day sharing how they worked and talked about the activities and outcomes from the initial pilot project. In the second half of the session CAMHs staff, including doctors, psychologists, psychotherapists and social workers, talked about the kinds of illnesses and conditions the young people involved in CAMHs present, how their service works, how the arts programme fits in with this structure and other interventions they use. Together the partners then explored the benefits for the young people involved and the future developments for the partnership.

" Children's services are driven by the need to achieve outcomes for children and young people. Galleries can help to contribute to this in many ways – through actual accredited outcomes for young people, to support for vulnerable groups and also support around actively engaging young people in the services for them. Quantifiable evidence is central to how children's services report against their planning and galleries need to ensure that they have the data to back up the work they do with young people. Children's services learn like most of us: experientially. The best way of showing these services what galleries have to offer is to provide them with as many different experiences as possible, to embed your organisation with their organisation and to provide young people with an opportunity to say what galleries mean to them "

Rachel Tranter, Head of Arts, Richmond Borough Council at Orleans House Gallery

'Sample Arts', Ikon Gallery, 2004

Working with hard to reach young people

envision has a particular focus on promoting the role galleries can play in building the skills, aspirations and engagement of young people at risk.

It can be argued that in those precarious teenage years all young people are potentially at risk. Young people generally lead chaotic lives but with particular groups the levels of motivation may be very low. Participants may be experiencing a range of difficult circumstances in their lives, only some of which you'll know about, and this may impact on their engagement with you. You'll need to be prepared and plan flexibly to accommodate this.

The five envision projects in the east region worked with very different groups of young people, for example Kings Lynn Arts Centre and Outpost Gallery targeted work with young people excluded from mainstream education and the Sainsbury Centre for Visual Arts developed work with a self-selected group including A level art students. Comparison between the groups brought into stark contrast significant differences in confidence and life experience:

It was shocking to think that they [young people] were of a similar age, living in a similar geographical area, but were experiencing such differences in social conditions, intellectual and creative ability and the ability to express their views.

Dr Jacqueline Watson, Enquire East: Learning for Empowerment, engage, 2007

For the galleries working with young people excluded from school the projects were very much about nurturing self-esteem, broadening their horizons and learning the elemental social and personal skills that more advantaged young people might learn from their families. Having a consistent link with the gallery was particularly beneficial in enabling those young people to feel reconnected and included in society.

❝When the boys first came to Kings Lynn Arts Centre their behaviour was particularly challenging; art educators encouraged the boys simply to play. By starting out with simple tasks like potato printing – the kind of thing children might normally do with their parents – their confidence grew. Needy young people, it took time and small steps to build their skills and encourage them to value their work and to learn to value themselves.**❞**

Dr Jacqueline Watson, Enquire East: Learning for Empowerment, engage, 2007

Jargon Buster

What envision means by the term **'at risk'** is those young people experiencing or at risk of disadvantage due to poverty, prejudice, isolation, family or personal circumstance. Other terms you may come across are: 'neet' (not in education employment or training), hard to reach, vulnerable, socially excluded, marginalised, disadvantaged.

'NR5 into Outpost', Outpost Gallery and Fruitful Arts, 2007

Why do you want to work with 'hard to reach' young people?

Be clear about your personal motivations for targeting vulnerable young people. Are you doing it just to chase funding or because you have a passion about this work? A lot of this will come down to your own personal integrity. Think about the ethics of what you're doing as well as the responsibility and the consequences. Be honest about your experience and skills and what you can realistically achieve.

Working with the most excluded groups can be both hugely rewarding and difficult. It requires a level of knowledge and experience – don't jump in at the deep end – get some experience and training, invest in building strong partnerships, employ experienced artists, plan properly and be prepared.

" Social inclusion programmes of work are not about levering money, keeping your local authority content, bums on seats or quick and dirty approaches. It takes time, energy and a great deal of thought to include not just the external parties but the whole organisation in the process. "

Clare Mitchell, Regional Youth Arts Officer, Regional Youth Work Unit, Government Office West Midlands

Tips on...
working with hard to reach young people

Rachel Tranter, Head of Arts, Richmond Borough Council at Orleans House Gallery

- Working with young people is very rewarding, particularly in an environment where we have had so much continuity in staffing that our young people can return to us over the years and continue to develop their relationship with us
- The experience is not all positive, but in some ways, the fact that we experience ups and the downs with our young people means that we are very much a part of their lives and a part of a sophisticated support structure of 'corporate parenting' with the local authority
- For young people to engage in galleries and for them to be creative, their basic needs must be met. You cannot work effectively with young people if they can't get to the gallery, or if they are hungry or if they are upset
- Once these needs are met it's really important to have very high expectations of our young people – there really is an issue about poverty of aspiration for vulnerable young people and it's our job to help them achieve beyond their expectations and the expectations of others
- For our young people the gallery is a place, like no other, where they can explore their creativity. Orleans is a safe place, where young people connect to their gallery 'family' and feel at home the usual suspects, you need to learn to read the signs

" I think we do it [work with hard to reach young people] because we like a challenge and I think we feel very strongly that when we work with these young people they've got no real parental support and often have stressful circumstances and, as just another human being, we feel compassion for them. Most people don't want to bother to work with them because they're hard work. I don't want to mention any names, but some of them already had ASBOs, some were hospitalising people, some just refused to attend school. And even from day one, once you start seeing their engagement it's really rewarding. **"**

Adult, Enquire East: Learning for Empowerment, engage, 2007

Working with youth services

Advice from Clare Mitchell, Regional Youth Arts Officer, Government Office West Midlands

The good thing about working with the youth service is that youth workers are excellent bridges for young people, they are familiar with working with young people in diverse settings and are used to challenging inappropriate behaviour. A good working relationship with a youth service can enable you to interact with young people on their terms, not as a pupil, but as an individual, and can provide supportive and experienced staff to help young people in accessing gallery provision.

Youth workers also have a wealth of knowledge about their local communities and know about legislation regarding children and young people. Youth services can also provide excellent training opportunities for gallery and museum staff.

By working with youth services your organisation can: contribute to the local authority youth offer, develop new audiences, challenge the preconceptions of what a gallery or museum can or should be, access work forcedevelopment, develop stronger links with local communities and develop and grow a variety of new work in partnership.

Things to consider

- Issues can arise when partnerships are not fully agreed, when youth workers themselves are uncomfortable or unfamiliar with your organisation's work or if youth workers have been drafted in to police or solve a 'youth problem' rather than to explore an opportunity
- Youth clubs have routine opening times; working outside of these times can be difficult to organise
- Be aware of other events and activities the youth service is providing to avoid clashes – particularly in the summer holidays
- Be prepared for a 'drop-in' environment and the lack of continuity of the group and plan your activity accordingly
- Youth workers may lack confidence and experience of the arts. Be clear about the project's purpose and the activity you're planning with all supporting staff
- Some key staff may work fixed hours and won't be able to come to planning meetings – make sure you have other ways of communicating details about the project to them

What you can do

Each local authority youth service in England will be organised in a slightly different way but each will have senior managers responsible for youth provision, including youth clubs and detached work in geographical areas. There will also be an Engagement or Participation Team that works across the local authority to support young people's inclusion and involvement in decision-making for youth provision. Your local authority will also be able to provide you with a list of independent youth groups in your area (such as faith or voluntary run groups). Also try contacting Regional Youth Arts Officers through your regional government office.

Jargon Buster

The youth service has a three-tier category to describe their engagement approaches:

Universal activity designed for and accessible by all young people

Targeted activity designed to target a specific demographic group, for example young offenders, young carers, young deaf people

Specific activity designed with a specific partner and a specific group of young people

Art Ambassadors

ProjectBase worked in partnership with detached youth workers on the streets in rural districts of Cornwall to discuss with young people arts provision in their area, with the idea of developing an art ambassadors scheme. The project was based around creating a 'conversation' with young people enabling planning of future initiatives to start with young people from the very beginning and for them to lead the process in their own way and at their own pace. The project has created new partnerships, new ideas and enthusiasm from young people about how they can make decisions about their own cultural provision.

"Approached in the best way – 100% definitely – being able to get to know the young people on an informal basis and with no expectation of them is essential in getting them involved. Having a good lead-in time to just talk directly to them and get to know them before asking them to commit to anything is great. There would have been little response if you had expected too much from them the first time you came. On the third session they were all approaching you and asking you questions which was great, you need to show an interest in the long-term and this has allowed you to do just that. "

Detached Youth Worker, Kerrier Youth Service

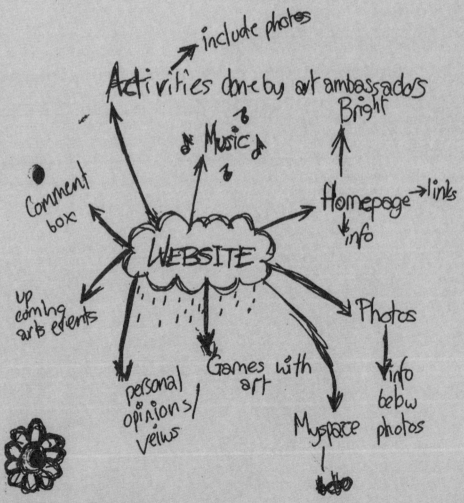

Wheelchair Users
Please wait here for evacuation
in the event of an emergency

LIFT
EZI

Working with disabled young people

Advice from Cath Hawes, Senior Arts Development Manager, Shape

Access is not just about the physical environment and physical 'aides' or intellectual access to art but also about emotional access. To address this issue it is important to:

- Allow for 'time-outs' and to provide quiet or separate spaces in which to do this
- Provide a safe environment to work in
- Manage expectation when working creatively with disabled children and young people
- Get everyone positively involved in all activities – parents, carers, teachers and support staff

Providing a safe environment is important in terms of enabling disabled children and young people to engage with and be creative in a gallery setting. Given that the gallery environment is usually predetermined by existing architecture and planning and therefore fairly inflexible, galleries and artists need to be imaginative in developing ways to provide a safe work setting.

If any young person (disabled or not) feels uncomfortable or insecure in an environment then focusing on a creative activity is inhibited by these feelings and sessions may be difficult to manage and comprehension and understanding may be impaired. Routine can play a part in establishing a safe environment – it's not always possible with time restrictions to develop a routine or pick up on individual learning needs and requirements, but liaising with a group before an activity is initiated can cover some of this ground in advance, which contributes to a more secure creative learning environment.

Working in this specific arena means changing your expectations not lowering them. It is important to be flexible in the way you gauge the success of a project or activity as it can be assessed using different criteria – that are no less indicative in measuring the impact of what you are doing – only the method of assessment is different. You need to be creative in evaluating achievement in terms of the activity and the audience.

Many organisations still shy away from working in this area – because of the 'fear' of the 'unknown', a perception that it is too difficult to deliver or requires too much time and effort for what is assumed to be minimal outcome. But we need to be aware that as inclusive education becomes more prevalent the nature of formal education groups will change. There will be fewer opportunities to work with discreet school groups as more young people become integrated into mainstream, as opposed to attending special needs schools. Therefore galleries will need to be more inclusive in nature, participants will have a broad range of needs that must be addressed during projects that are accessible to all.

'Young Vision', Scarborough Arts Gallery, 2007

Jargon Buster

The **Social Model of Disability** was developed by disabled people to identify and take action against discrimination. It is a challenge to the notion of disability as an individual, medical 'problem' which focuses on what the disabled person can't do, because of their impairment. This approach, known as the **Medical Model of Disability**, can be unhelpful and dehumanising.

The Social Model sees disability as something that is socially constructed. Disability is created by physical, organisational and attitudinal barriers and these can be changed or removed. It stops 'blaming' the individual for their shortcomings and argues that impairment is and always will be present in every known society, so we should be planning in a way that includes, rather than excludes, disabled people. The Social Model makes a clear distinction between impairment (the condition, illness or loss/lack of function) and disability (barriers and discrimination).

Medical
Individual
What's wrong with you?
Justification

Social
Environment
What are the barriers here?
Information on a need to know basis

Case study:

Inside Outside

North West Disability Arts Forum (NWDAF) and Tate Liverpool worked together to research the requirements of young disabled and deaf people in attending programmes and events, particularly Young Tate – the gallery's programme for young people aged 14-25 years old. Non-disabled peer leaders from Young Tate acted as mentors for the group, 'buddying-up' with individual participants. They acted as guides around the venue, showing the disabled young people where things were and introducing them to groups and activities. This provided experience for the young people acting as mentors and a familiar face to greet the disabled young people when making return visits. Through the project a number of recommendations for good practice emerged and fed into plans to develop these relationships further. Suggestions included: reviewing access strategies as an ongoing process – the more Tate works with disabled young people the more they are learning and gaining an awareness of how to improve access, including resources and staff training; consulting with participants of Young Tate first to help them understand the changes that may take place, why it was happening and the needs of the new members. A full copy of the recommendations by project artist and co-ordinator, Ross Clark, can be found on the envision website under Resources at www.en-vision.org.uk

" My ideas were good and people liked them. "

Young person

Resources for creative work with disabled young people

- Use resources that are based on case studies and examples of best practice rather than physical models of disability
- Work with and learn from artists/educators experienced in working creatively with young people
- Have a working knowledge of the Social Model of Disability. Consider the barriers to accessing creative practice rather than what a disabled young person is perceived to be able to do (or not do) by society and Medical Models of Disability
- A written guide or 'toolbox', whilst useful, can never cover every eventuality you may experience. Asking questions, networking, picking up on successful ideas and getting out there and doing it is the best way of informing what you do

What you can do

Contact your local authority Education and Learning department for details of education provision for young people with special educational needs (SEN), including special schools. They should also have a list of other organisations which provide services outside of school for disabled children and young people in your area.

Contact Shape (the UK's leading disability arts organisation) for best practice models, training, resources and contacts for experienced practitioners. Go to www.shapearts.org.uk

Jargon Buster

The **Disability Discrimination Act (DDA)** 1995 gives rights to people who currently have or have had in the past an impairment which is 'substantial and adverse and makes it difficult for them to carry out normal day to day activities.' Impairments can be physical, sensory or mental. It must also have a long-term effect (that means the impairment must last or be expected to last for 12 months or more). Conditions which have a slight effect on day-to-day activities, but are expected to become substantial are covered. Severe disfigurement is also included within the definition.

It is estimated that approximately 10 million people in the UK are covered by this definition. The DDA requires all service providers to make 'reasonable adjustments' to ensure their services and recruitment opportunities are accessible to deaf and disabled people. No matter what the size of your organisation is, if you employ any staff or if you provide any service then the DDA applies to YOU!

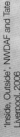

'Inside, Outside', NWDAF and Tate Liverpool, 2006

Working with young people at risk of offending

If you are planning to work with young people at risk of offending you should already have experience of working with vulnerable young people. You should ideally also work with professionals who work with young people at risk of offending, such as your local youth offending service or neighbouhood crime provention workers. The project may need to fit into their established practice but is likely to benefit considerably from tried and tested strategies to meet individual needs, manage behaviour and evaluate outcomes.

Be aware that the young people attending may be there because they have to, perhaps as part of a court order, as this will affect their motivation and behaviour. You will need to focus on keeping activities fun and interactive to win them over. Be aware that literacy levels tend to be low and that you're more likely to be working with young men.

This area of work is currently a priority for the Arts Council and they have been developing a national partnership and strategy with the Youth Justice Board, including initiatives such as the PLUS Arts Enrichment Programme, Summer Art Colleges, Arts and Youth Offending Teams (YOTs) regional posts, conferences and training opportunities.

What you can do

Each local authority has a Youth Offending Team. See the YJB website to find out local contacts at www.yjb.gov.uk. Contact your Arts Council regional office to find out how the PLUS strategy is being implemented in your area.

Straight Talking

Fabrica, in partnership with Brighton & Hove Youth Offending Team, focused on developing partnership working between the ISSP (Intense Supervision and Surveillance Programme) and the gallery through the exchange of knowledge and skills between a small group of young offenders, two Fabrica education staff, three education volunteers, an artist and one Youth Justice Officer.

The project comprised mentoring, joint planning and team building activities including five 'familiarisation' sessions where the Fabrica team worked alongside young people and youth justice workers on a gardening activity to get some first-hand experience of working with participants in a situation that Fabrica didn't have to manage. This built staff confidence and informed the planning of a series of photography workshops where the young people worked one-to-one with a Fabrica volunteer or staff member as co-participant. Young people were encouraged to adopt a positive, self-determined approach and their comments fed into future planning. Fabrica now has a better understanding of working with young offenders and developed ideas about how to take this partnership forward.

'Straight Talking', Fabrica, 2007

"The success of these kinds of organisational partnerships actually depends on good communication between key individuals, a joint commitment to make the project happen and mutual respect of each others' professional practice. Once this is in place projects can be developed as a genuine collaboration. Undertaking the [envision] research project – both preparing for it and working directly with the young people – challenged our pre-conceived ideas about their attitudes and behaviour. It gave us space to observe, listen and learn, and to discuss our concerns and plan strategies for working with the young people. It supported us in becoming more confident about working with young offenders. Pairing up volunteers with the young people worked well as it gave the young people one-to-one attention with someone not much older than them and helped counteract/deflect disruptive behaviour. The volunteers – who were all under 25 years old – developed good relationships with the young people and really enjoyed the sessions. They felt well prepared and supported in the project. "

Liz Whitehead, Co-Director, Fabrica

'Straight Talking', Fabrica, 2007

Jargon Buster

YJB – Youth Justice Board. The YJB oversees the youth justice system in England and Wales to prevent offending by children and young people under the age of 18, and to ensure that custody for them is safe, secure and addresses the causes of their offending behaviour.

YOT or YOS – Youth Offending Teams or Services. YOTs identify the needs of each young offender by assessing them, finding out the specific problems that make the young person offend, the risk they pose to others and suitable programmes to prevent further offending.

PLUS – The YJB PLUS strategy aims to raise literacy and numeracy levels of children and young people in order to prevent crime. It delivers resources, training and projects including the summer arts schools and arts champions initiatives.

ASBO – Anti-Social Behaviour Orders are used against anyone who is 10 years old or over and has behaved in a manner that caused or was likely to cause harassment, alarm or distress to someone or some people who do not live in their own household.

ISO – Individual Support Order. ISOs are court orders for 10-17 year olds which can be attached to 'stand alone' ASBOs and impose positive conditions on a young person to address the underlying causes of the behaviour that led to the ASBO. They can last up to six months and can require a young person to attend up to two sessions a week under the supervision of the YOT.

ISSP – Intensive Supervision and Surveillance Programme is the most rigorous non-custodial intervention available for young offenders. It combines community based surveillance with a focus on tackling the factors that contribute to the young person's offending behaviour.

YISP – Youth Inclusion and Support Panel. Targeted support for 8–13 year olds identified as being at risk of offending, inluding, for example, a creative project diverting attention from less positive activities.

RAP – Resettlement and Prevention programme. Aftercare support for people leaving custody. Potentially including creative activity.

"The UK is bottom of the league of 21 economically advanced countries according to UNICEF on the well-being of children and adolescents. Nowhere is this more acutely evident than in the complex world of youth justice. For over 30 years the dominant strand of museum and gallery initiatives has been focused around formal learning, yet so much of this practice directly appeals to ideas of welfare, identity and society – key drivers for success when working with this target group."

Richard Beales, Outreach and Inclusion Manager, Towner Art Gallery

Working with alternative education providers

Alternative education providers include Pupil Referral Units and Learning Support Units, Entry to Employment (E2E) courses and Alternative Provision for young people excluded or at risk of school exclusion.

For young people whose school life is usually an experience of failure and frustration, galleries can provide a great alternative learning experience and involve them in opportunities to achieve and to celebrate their work in a public space, get recognition and to contribute something to their community.

Be aware that working with alternative education providers usually means that the young people won't have volunteered to attend your project – it will be part of the curriculum. Much of the guidance given around working with young people at risk of offending also applies to working with young people excluded from mainstream education.

What you can do

Each local authority Education Service will have contacts for Pupil Referral Units and any other alternative education services for young people permanently excluded or at risk of exclusion from school. Many schools also have an internal unit to support additional learning needs and behavioural issues for pupils.

E2E is a national initiative managed by regional Learning and Skills Councils to offer young people aged 16–18 years old, not in education, training or employment, a course in basic skills and work-based learning opportunities.

Also try NOPRU (National Organisation for Pupil Referral Units) at www.prus.org.uk or arts.prus.org.uk

"Creative activities allow for more self expression than most curriculum subjects and this means that young people in these settings (PRUs) can achieve something which is theirs, which says who they are and how they feel about the world. This in turn begins to build up their confidence, which is often so damaged. It creates the feeling: 'This is me and I am doing it.'**"**

Simon Richie

Links 4

Kings Lynn Arts Centre in partnership with the Rosebury Centre Pupil Referral Unit involved three young men working with an animated film artist to create their own short animated films. Although the artistic medium of the project was prescribed, the story and the filming process were led by participants.

Each young man wrote his own storyboard and made figures and props from Plasticene and sets for the action to take place. They filmed their animated story adding sound effects and titles. The films were exhibited as part of the *en-titled* exhibition at the Sainsbury Centre for Visual Arts in Norwich. Participants started attending on a voluntary basis in their free time and used their new-found skills, including leading an arts workshop with a local primary school, to achieve the Bronze Arts Award. One young man now has a year-long, day a week work placement at the Arts Centre.

" This is something we don't have to do, but we enjoy it. We don't have to be here. It's just a thing we choose to do. [I didn't notice the art] as much as I do now. I've got more into the feeling of how interesting it is. Before it was just an old painting on the wall. It's made a difference, coming here. "

Participant, Links 4

'Links 4', Kings Lynn Arts Centre 2007

Working with schools

Advice from Barbara Taylor, Programme Director, enquire

There is a lot of evidence about the wide range of benefits to teachers, children and young people of working with galleries. The most important is the opportunity to see real works of art in a gallery context. A relationship with a gallery – and often with an artist – also brings an understanding of the 'process' of making a creative intervention, an increased understanding about cultural institutions and about the role of art in our professional, social, economic and personal life.

It is found that galleries, vitally, offer a different site for learning, which is separate and different to the constraints and conventions of the school and which is outside the labels and judgements sometimes applied in school.

Not surprisingly, the more discussion and planning that takes place between the gallery educator and teacher, the more successful the visit or project. This often means that the teacher will do work in advance and after the project. The students are better prepared for the experience and the teacher develops knowledge, confidence and skills to make use of the resource on an ongoing basis.

To continue working with schools in a meaningful way galleries do have to demonstrate the relevance of working with art across the curriculum. While the Extended Schools, Arts Awards and other initiatives can bring schools into contact with galleries, it is necessary to embed working in galleries as a part of the standard curriculum delivery for a wide range of subjects. The school's directive Working Outside the Classroom manifesto encourages this and galleries have to demonstrate that they can deliver relevant, exciting and innovative programmes for students within the normal curriculum.

There are many policies and initiatives to encourage schools to engage with galleries. Gallery education has been shown to make a valuable contribution to over-arching educational objectives such as developing creativity, supporting personalised and self-directed learning, and teaching citizenship, along with encouraging greater civic participation.

In more specific terms, schools should view galleries as a fundamental and normal resource for the teaching of art and design at all levels, as argued by Ian Middleton, HMI Specialist Advisor for Art and Design, Ofsted: 'Standards and achievement are higher where pupils engage with original art through first-hand experience of work with artists, galleries and, more significantly, both together.'

What you can do

Your local authority website should list Education and Learning Services or Children's Services. Some local authorities have an Arts in Education Team, or equivalent and you might also find specific teams working with refugee and ethnic minority groups, traveller groups and young people in care.

Keep up to date with Creative Partnerships initiatives and resources at www.creative-partnerships.com

Get a copy of the *Watch this Space Toolkit* and handbook, *Watch this Space: Galleries and schools in partnership*. See www.engage.org/publications for more details.

Tips on…
working with schools

Penny Jones, Watch this Space Co-ordinator

- Offer attractive, enjoyable training and introductory events to teachers which emphasise the high quality of your collections and exhibitions and their relevance to work in school
- Prepare yourself. Research the school you are going to work with so that you can negotiate with knowledge and know what the National Curriculum requirements are for students
- Be flexible and open and allow plenty of planning time
- Consult with teachers about their students' needs. Work together to devise programmes and projects, and be prepared to go into school to meet teachers and students
- Keep teachers informed of exhibitions and events through different marketing approaches
- Seek support from the school's management. Individual teachers with enthusiasm and commitment are very important in building relationships with galleries but the head teacher and senior management team have to be involved and support the partnership in order to make it sustainable over a period of time. This support provides a strategic overview for the partnership that can extend involvement in gallery education to a range of subjects, and can bring in funding from education and arts sources to enable the partnership to grow
- Respect and acknowledge teachers' expertise and their knowledge of their students
- Take on the responsibility for arranging meetings, recording and feeding back information
- Choose who you work with carefully. Not all schools are ready to take on a partnership with you – this does not mean just work with the usual suspects, you need to learn to read the signs

Art Ambassadors II

ProjectBase, working in partnership with Newlyn Gallery, Equality & Diversity Services (Children's Services Authority Cornwall) and Poltair School, St Austell, created the opportunity for open dialogue with a group of young people about what they want, need and require from local galleries and public art projects. The group consisted of seven English as additional language (EAL) students and three English first language (EFL) students. ProjectBase facilitated the sharing of ideas, thoughts, views and opinions about the contemporary visual arts through youth-led processes. This included gallery visits and creative collaborations with artists including an Argentinian artists' collective working in residence at Newlyn's Exchange Gallery and who shared the same first language as the EAL students.

The project has created an open dialogue with 10 young people who were recognised as non-gallery attending, and explored working with participants and artists who speak English as an additional language. The scope of the project embraced their first languages, discovering new approaches to best practice for equality and diversity awareness.

❝The school has recognised the value to students and in particular the integration between EAL and EFL students. The improvement in students' well-being and attitude to work has exceeded the expectations of staff supporting the project. They have stated that they want to continue working in partnership with ProjectBase in the next academic year.❞

Dodie Bridges, Project Coordinator, ProjectBase

Different approaches to involving young people

Below you'll find some ideas to give you inspiration. This is by no means an exhaustive list, but it is a list of real examples from arts venues involved in envision which are actively involving young people in their work.

Youth advisory and programming groups

Thelma Hulbert Gallery
Young people meet to advise on signage, usage of the space, and programming to attract more visitors.

Manchester Art Gallery
The Creative Consultants help to interpret artworks for a young audience through events, trails or activities within the Exhibitions and Collections galleries.

Sainsbury Centre for Visual Arts
The peer-led enquire group of young art students identify ways the centre can contribute to their professional development and advise the organisation on ways to encourage more young visitors through gallery interpretation, exhibitions and recruitment to sustain the group.

ProjectBase, Cornwall
The Arts Ambassadors scheme facilitates opportunities and training for children and young people to be involved in the development and delivery of their programmes.

Getting ideas

Making artworks and developing young people's critical/cultural understanding

Metropole Gallery
The LivingArt project focused on introducing young people to new cultural experiences, creative making and thinking, and a purpose built studio space/ installation within the gallery to share their ideas and self-expression with others.

Youth designed websites

The Royal Pumprooms, Leamington Spa
Working in partnership with Warwickshire Youth Arts Network developed a 'what's on' website for young people living in rural Warwickshire.

The Study Gallery, Poole
Working with the Bournemouth & Poole Cultural Hub, young people designed and managed the Hubalicious website, which showcases and reviews creative work by young people and has information on events, gigs and career opportunities in the cultural sector.

Exhibitions and interpretation

Manchester Art Gallery
The Creative Consultants worked with the exhibition team to co-curate the *Disguise* exhibition, choosing artists, painting the walls deep purple and designing a resource space and interactive comments screen.

Babylon Gallery, Ely
Set up an Ely open exhibition and encouraged young people on the gallery's Arts Awards scheme to submit and sell their work.

Youth-led happenings and events in a gallery space

Spacex, Exeter
The X-Panel group of young people invited local young bands to perform in the gallery space.

Sainsbury Centre for Visual Arts, Norwich
The enquire young people's group organised public interventions and happenings in the gallery space.

Young person's work from the Babylon Gallery at the 'entitled' exhibition, Enquire _ Envision East Cluster at the Sainsbury Centre for Visual Arts, 2008. Photo Andi Sapey

Young people co-delivering training and professional development

Ikon Gallery, Birmingham
Arts professionals, youth workers and young people explored ways of making the gallery more accessible. Activities included joint training, skill sharing and devising and sampling gallery workshops.

Nottingham Castle Museum and Gallery
Young people from the Wordz Out project facilitated activities for gallery educators at the envision, *Beyond Marketing* seminar in 2005.

Young people as gallery guides

The Photographers' Gallery, London
The Teen Talks programme supports young people to research, develop and deliver public talks in the gallery.

Angel Row Gallery, Nottingham
Young people researched and designed a DVD and booklet for gallery staff and visitors about their findings and ideas on accessing contemporary arts.

Young people as peer mentors to other young people

North West Disability Arts Forum worked with **Tate Liverpool** to develop a programme where Young Tate Leaders supported disabled young people to access and engage with the gallery.

Young people fundraising for their own youth programme

Cornerhouse, Manchester
The Livewire programme is run by a management team of young people who work with the Young People's Programme Manager to design, fundraise for and implement a young people's programme.

Work experience placements and volunteering

Kings Lynn Arts Centre
Offered a year-long work placement to a young person in partnership with a local pupil referral unit.

198 Gallery, London
Developed a work-based learning volunteer scheme, which offers young people opportunities to work alongside gallery professionals.

'Sample Arts',
Ikon Gallery, 2004

Galleries facilitating young people's involvement in wider agendas

Orleans House Gallery, Richmond
Developed a programme of creative consultation to input into and help communicate with local young people, the details of the Local Area Agreement for Children's Services in Richmond.

Bow Arts Trust, London
Worked with local regeneration schemes to develop proposals for a new arts education building in the community.

Young people delivering workshops to other young people

Kings Lynn Arts Centre
Young people shared their new skills by delivering workshops to local primary school children for their Bronze Arts Award.

Supporting GCSE art qualifications

Orleans House Gallery, Richmond
The gallery has become a registered centre for delivering GCSE art to young people struggling in mainstream education.

Outpost Gallery, Norwich
Worked in partnership with Fruitful Arts and NR5 alternative education centre to devise sessions using Outpost Gallery's space and exhibitions to support GCSE art students' work.

Creating online opportunities for young people

Kings Lynn Arts Centre
Established an online gallery encouraging young people and other emerging artists to exhibit.

Sainsbury Centre for Visual Arts, Norwich
has created pages on My Space and Bebo with young people.

Young people as auditors for a gallery's youth-friendliness

Scarborough Art Gallery
Young people explored the gallery and gave feedback on their thoughts and ideas to the gallery staff and visitors via discussion and installation pieces in the gallery space.

Manchester Art Gallery
Young people worked with gallery staff and a filmmaker to create a visual audit of the gallery's services and programmes for young people.

Imagine a world or workplace where you have the money to do all the things you want. A world where your manager says: 'Here have a large sum of money' on a regular basis. Not your world? Then read on.

Working with young people does not need to be expensive and you can achieve a lot with your time and the use of the space and resources to hand. However, if you have bigger ambitions you will inevitably have to seek some form of funding. Examples of things requiring funding might be the cost of commissioning artists to work with young people, support and access costs, transport, materials and your time. Where you go for this funding depends on what it is for and how much you want. The good news is that there are plenty of funding sources out there. The bad news is that it is a very competitive market with a lot of organisations after the same pots of money.

The first approach for funding could be your own organisation. On the basis of 'if you don't ask you don't get' it is worth making the case for funding for work with young people. Use the information in the first section of this handbook to justify your case. If you can secure an amount of money, however big or small, this may be enough to cover the work you want to carry out or to use as match funding for funding applications.

Where to go for up-to-date information on funding sources

If your organisation can't supply the required funds you will need to approach other sources. Some of the most common of these are government, National Lottery, Arts Council, trusts and foundations, international funds and business.

A good starting point is to contact the arts development team at your local or district authority. They should be able to provide information on local, regional and national funding opportunities and priorities.

The Department of Culture, Media and Sport (DCMS) produces an annual Guide to Arts Funding in England. The purpose of the guide is to 'help artists and arts organisations navigate their way around the arts funding system in England and to identify specific funding opportunities'. It does what it says on the tin and is therefore a highly recommended resource. To download the current version go to the DCMS website at www.culture.gov.uk and type 'guide to arts funding' into the search bar.

If you will be regularly looking for funding it may be worth investing in a specialist publication or a subscription to receive regular funding information updates. The DCMS guide gives details of some of the most useful ones relating to the arts in the publications section at the end of the document.

Some of the best publications on the subject of fundraising come from the Directory of Social Change which is a registered charity and the major provider of information and training to the voluntary sector. It publishes over 300 titles on fundraising and organises specialist courses and conferences. Go to www.dsc.org.uk

The publications section on the DSC website includes a number of relevant titles such as:

Youth Funding Guide
by Nicola Eastwood

Arts Funding Guide
by Susan Forrester and David Lloyd

Cultural Giving
by Theresa Lloyd

Directory of Grant Making Trusts 2007-08
by Alan French, Sarah Johnston, Denise Lillya, John Smythe

A Guide to the Major Trusts Volume 1, 2007-08
by Tom Traynor and Denise Lilly

A Guide to the Major Trusts Volume 2, 2007-08
by Alan French & John Smyth

Tips on...
Filling in a Funding Application

- Make sure you follow the instructions! It sounds obvious but it is surprising how many applications fail at the first hurdle as they simply have not answered the questions or have not enclosed the required information.
- Make your overview or summary of the project clear and exciting – you want your application to stand out. Give it to someone else to read, preferably not connected with your work, and ask for their response.
- Be clear about what you want to achieve (limit to one aim) and what specific actions you will take to achieve this (about five objectives).
- Include cash and in-kind contributions in your budget, and make sure the income and expenditure balance (it's surprising how many people make this mistake).
- Consider evaluation and documentation from the outset. For larger applications you may think about commissioning an external evaluator and a professional photographer.

Jargon Buster

The majority of funders will not provide 100% of the cost of a project and will require some form of **match funding**. Most funding applications will state the percentage of match funding required and will indicate if this needs to be 'cash' or whether it can be 'in kind'.

In kind funding refers to resources and services that are provided by partners, such as staff time, venue costs, equipment and materials. For example: provision of meeting space 10 hours X £20 = £200, line management fee 4 days @ £120 = £480.

Even if match funding is not requested it is a good idea to show where either cash or in kind contributions will be made as it demonstrates your commitment to the work.

You have to pay for them but the cost is low in relation to the invaluable information they provide and they will save you a great deal of time helping you direct your efforts. Two examples of sources for regularly updated advice and information are Funding Digest and FunderFinder.

Funding Digest produces a funding newsletter every two months by subscription. It is worth contacting your local authority or library to see if they subscribe or contact Funding Digest direct to see if there are any multi-use subscriptions in your area.

Funding Digest
RTI Publications
St Mary's Centre
Suite 102, Oystershell Lane
Newcastle upon Tyne NE4 5QS
0191 232 6942
Email chris@rtipub.co.uk

FunderFinder is a small UK charity producing software and other resources, mainly for grant-seekers. They specialise in information and advice about charitable trusts and foundations that fund in the UK. Their website address is www.funderfinder.org.uk. The website has some really useful advice leaflets, software downloads and a 'jargon buster'. Some elements are free and some have to be paid for.

Young people's involvement

Providers of funding for work with young people increasingly require evidence that young people have had significant involvement in the development of applications. This obviously makes great sense. One word of caution however would be to ensure that you manage the expectations of the young people you work with as there are no guarantees that the applications will be successful.

Organisational restrictions

Your organisation may already receive funding from a particular source that excludes you from applying for further funds. Discuss with your management or accounting staff which funding sources to go for. If your organisation's funding structure restricts you from making certain applications you could consider working with a partner organisation and getting them to make the application.

Building a track record

If you are asking for large sums of money most funders will want to see some sort of track record to demonstrate that you have the capability of managing projects of that scale. If you do not have a track record consider asking for a smaller amount to carry out pilot work or a feasibility study. This can then feed into a larger project in the future. If possible try and build up a relationship with a representative from the funding body and get some advice on your plans.

Some useful funding websites

www.fundraising.co.uk
www.access-funds.co.uk
www.governmentfunding.org.uk
www.grantnet.com
www.uksponsorship.com
www.trustfunding.org.uk

NR5 into Outpost, Outpost Gallery and Fruitful Arts, 2007

Project planning

You will need to plan effectively and clearly in order to deliver a good project and to be able to evaluate it afterwards. The two activities are inextricably linked and they both start from being clear about what the project is intended to do.

Planning is a normal part of any project cycle and most arts professionals are used to doing it. Good planning can greatly improve a project's viability and impact. Hours spent thinking things through can save days of frustration and misunderstanding.

But the quality of planning is variable, partly because most of it happens in response to a funding opportunity: the plans reflect what might get financed, not always what should get done and there are often gaps where the application form didn't ask certain questions.

A common weakness in arts project planning is in the aim and objectives. This is often vague, overambitious, naïve or unrealistic – in short, not much use as a guide for the project. As a result, people often ignore the aim and objectives when actually delivering the work. This can lead to various problems, but the one that matters here is the difficulty of evaluating a project that isn't clear about what it's trying to do or doesn't do what it says.

Good evaluation depends on a clear link between what was intended and what has happened: how you show that the project has been effective. Too often people do a project they have thought up with vague aspirations about its results and then go on a fishing expedition for anything positive that might justify what happened. That's not evaluation – it's covering your back.

What is evaluation?

Before looking in more detail at aims – how you define the project's purpose – it's worth clarifying what we mean by evaluation. The first thing is that it's not monitoring, which is intended to show whether contracts have been delivered to a satisfactory standard. Monitoring can show what activity has happened, but not what the results were, nor, more importantly, what their value was.

Evaluation is concerned not just with accounting for funds but with understanding what has happened, how and why it has happened and the insights or knowledge that can be drawn from it. Ultimately, it's also concerned with deciding what the value of something is – whether the results justify the effort and resources used. That is always a judgement: there is no universal benchmark. But good evaluation will make those judgements better and more objective.

What is the purpose of evaluation?

Evaluation has become commonplace in arts administration in the past 10 or 15 years. At best that has introduced greater accountability into funding agreements, at worst it has produced a vast amount of unreliable and unread reporting and a considerable waste of time.

Evaluation shouldn't be done in the hope of proving an activity's worth or the wisdom of a spending decision. It should be done to gain knowledge about your work, test practice and help improve it. It has to be done honestly or not at all. Look for the problems and the failures as much as the successes. Look for why something has happened, not just what happened.

Don't confuse evaluation with advocacy: they're different things. Evaluation is about understanding and learning, not persuasion. It may provide evidence you can use in advocating your work but it will not usually convince sceptics of its value. Experience is much more persuasive. If you want to build support for your work, try to give your stakeholders direct experience of what you do. See Wrapping Up for ideas about how you can promote your work to others.

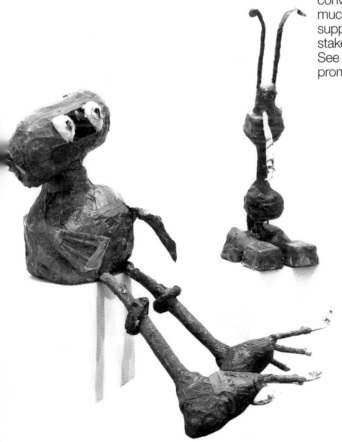

Young people's work from NR5 at the *entitled* exhibition, enquire envision east cluster at the Sainsbury Centre for Visual Arts, 2008 photo by Andy Crouch

Project aims and objectives

The starting point of the process is to establish what the activity is intending to achieve. Whatever else emerges from the evaluation, it must be able to report on progress against goals. A project's aim and objectives is important because it states what people are hoping to achieve and how they intend to go about it. It doesn't need to be long, bureaucratic or laced with jargon. On the contrary, it should be clear to everyone involved and memorable enough to be used in everyday explanations of the project's purpose.

The objectives should describe the main activities being undertaken to achieve the aim. They should include everything which is essential to achieving it and nothing which isn't.

Here are two examples of clear aim and objective statements from two very different envision projects:

Fabrica Straight Talking

Aim
The aim of the project is to increase access to contemporary art for young people in Brighton & Hove on the Intensive Supervision and Surveillance Programme (ISSP).

Objectives
- By holding four to six activity sessions for six to 10 young people on the ISSP programme, which will broaden their experience and skills through engagement with contemporary art and ideas
- By supporting gallery staff and volunteers to work with these young people through supervised familiarisation, training and other CPD activities
- By giving staff the knowledge and experience to make appropriate organisational change for future access and partnership
- By exploring the potential of the project's results to be used for advocacy

Thelma Hulbert Gallery KickstART

Aim
The aim of the project is to increase young people's participation in the gallery

Objectives
- By evaluating how many young people are already involved in the gallery
- By recruiting approximately 10 young people to the project
- By consulting with young people about making the gallery youth-friendly
- By organising a programme of activities for young people
- By developing a structure for the youth panel and youth volunteering to continue after the project has finished

Each objective can be expanded to include detailed plans about tasks, targets and assumptions, in keeping with various common planning and management practices. What detail you need, will depend on the project's scale and complexity. This model can be applied to the strategic aims of an organisation or to a long-term programme, as well as to an individual project. A simple, clear and agreed statement of aim and objectives is essential to project evaluation: unless you know what you are trying to achieve, you have no way to assess your progress.

Indicators

Once you have a clear statement of what you are going to do (aim) and how you are going to do it (objectives) you can begin to think about how you will know when and how far it has been achieved. You can identify indicators for each element of a project, including:

- Inputs (what was invested)
- Outputs (what was produced)
- Standards (how well it was done)
- Outcomes (what the results were)

So, for a gallery education project, you might use these indicators:

- Staff time and costs (inputs)
- Sessions delivered, attendances, work produced (outputs)
- Artists and tutors' qualifications, participants' satisfaction, quality of work (standards)
- Acquisition of new skills and confidence by the participants, new friendships, improved school attendance, independent visits to the gallery by young people (outcomes)

Impact indicators

Assessing the impact of your work can be tricky. For some things, such as whether the young people come back to the gallery after the project, it may be quite straightforward to attribute that to your work. But in the case of projects with wider ambitions, such as getting young people back into mainstream education or reducing offending, the links may be harder to prove.

Is the fact that a young person is back in school clearly and uniquely attributable to their participation in the project?

Is their failure to go back attributable to weaknesses in the project or are external factors (such as their family situation) the actual cause?

Did they go back as a result of what the project offered? There will usually have been other factors at play.

Is the desired outcome, ie returning to education, proportionate with the project's offer, ie the time, resources and content invested?

Be careful about placing unreasonably high expectations on short arts projects. You should be cautious when setting indicators for project impact. In most cases the more easily managed (and perhaps more reliable) indicators for inputs, outputs, standards and outcomes will be sufficient for evaluation.

Jargon Buster

A project's **aim** should be: a clear statement of purpose, a self-explanatory statement, shaped by values, communicable (understood by everyone) and memorable.

A project's **objectives** should: describe how to achieve this aim, set out intended action, enable essential work to happen, provide a structure for detailed planning, summarise the project.

Indicators help us measure to what extent our aim has been met.

Choosing indicators

Indicators should be specific to projects or organisations. So you will need to develop indicators for your work which are appropriate to your own objectives and expressed in language which reflects your own values and preoccupations.

How to measure if your aim has been met

To help you plan your own work, here are some outcome indicators suggested by gallery educators involved in the envision programme:

- Number of activity/mentoring sessions delivered
- Audit of current experience/new experience/ skills achieved
- Changes in young people's attitudes
- Confidence audit for participants and staff – before and after the project
- Young people's attendance at activities or events, their involvement and participation or levels of enthusiasm and confidence
- Number of ideas tested
- Young people willing and able to discuss their views openly
- Young people's independent and/or sustained access to the gallery and other new spaces
- Successful partnership achieved and/or continued
- Change in attitude/policy/practice of your organisation after the project

Who decides?

All of this raises one fundamental question: who sets the aim and objectives? Ideally, it will be a shared process, involving all the stakeholders (people who can affect or be affected by the project).

In practice that's unlikely to happen, at least at the outset. You may not be able to engage others until you have a project that they can see it is worth being part of: young people in particular are unlikely to want to take part in such discussions before they have been involved in a rewarding creative process. Some stakeholders may not be interested in talking about aims: they may just want you to make a proposal that they will choose to be involved in – or not.

All this matters because, whether they know it or not, all the stakeholders will have expectations from the project. Those expectations are why they are prepared to be involved. If they are not articulated in the aim and objectives, they may emerge later when people discover that what they thought was going to happen didn't. Furthermore, if they're not in the aim and objectives, they may not get observed or reported on, so things that are important to some people are effectively ignored in the evaluation.

There isn't an easy solution to this. The more times you go through the project cycle with a group of stakeholders, the better they will understand the process and share control of it. But in the early stages try to be aware of different stakeholders' expectations and try to take account of them in the work.

Building in planning and evaluation

Building evaluation into project development isn't difficult. It's largely a matter of taking a methodical approach to existing good practice. Specifically, it means:

- Agreeing with stakeholders what the project is intended to achieve
- Testing proposed plans against the aim and objectives
- Identifying indicators of success and ways of monitoring them
- Implementing work and recording data about progress
- Reviewing the results and reporting back

Remember you'll need to have an evaluation plan in place before you start the project so you can start capturing the evidence from day one.

See Wrapping up for more information about evaluation methods, tracking change and reporting and learning.

Notes

Doing it

Jo Wheeler

Projects that involve the active participation of young people and partnerships can be complex. We can't say 'this situation will always be like this and here's what to do about it' but in this section we offer guidance for working with young people, working with a project team and best practice advice on what you should consider in managing your project safely.

If we want young people to feel that galleries have something to offer them as visitors, participants or volunteers then we need to involve young people directly in the process and view this as a two-way relationship with potential barriers, benefits and learning for both young people and galleries.

We need to acknowledge young people may have barriers to accessing our venues – and our venues may have barriers in engaging with young people.

There are a number of principles, legal child protection, health and safety and confidentiality considerations that you must ensure are in place when working with young people. Once these are addressed the best way to work with either groups or individual young people is to talk to them.

But don't underestimate the time it will take. If you want to genuinely involve young people in decision-making at your gallery it will take time, commitment and resources, but even seemingly very small steps, if done well, will begin a relationship, have value and could build the foundations for something more ambitious.

Although we're talking about working with 'young people' as a demographic group it's really important to remember that young people are individuals and are just as different and complex as the rest of us.

Which is why when programming work with a group of young people it's really important to get to know them as individuals and discover their own interests, ambitions, strengths, needs, skills and abilities. We shouldn't assume that all young people are into graffiti and DJ-ing and make the most of our unique collections.

Be aware that by consulting with a small group you will gain valuable insights into aspects of youth culture and be able to start addressing the basic barriers to access, but be realistic: this will not enable your programme to cater for every local young person.

Tips on…
working with young people

Johnny Gailey, Opt in for Art Co-ordinator, Fruitmarket Gallery

- Devise a programme of activity for all young people – targeted projects must always feed off, and into, a wider open programme and not stand alone. A open universal provision provides the foundation for effective work with targeted groups

- Don't define young people by their 'issue', or their 'problem' – it's not up to us to define that or worse try and solve it. Start from the basis that all young people have potential which we want to develop in an open-ended way

- Always put the young people and their interests first – focus on what the gallery can do for young people, rather than what the young people can do for the gallery

- Establish a direct and respectful relationship where the young people can challenge you, by challenging the young people

- The young people should decide for themselves if they want to take part or if they want to walk away – have a alternative space, such as a café, for individual young people to go to if they wish to disengage

- It's okay if they don't like the artwork – it's not about convincing them otherwise. Leave room for their own interpretation – don't be prescriptive about the artwork

- Always present with a lively mind. Be receptive, make connections and follow young people's ideas and responses – the job is to draw stuff out of the young people

- Make it fun. It's not what you are saying that's important, it's what they are hearing

" The young people on the Opt in for Art programme were given control to develop their own projects, to represent themselves and only themselves, rather than to speak on behalf of young people per se. "

Johnny Gailey, Fruitmarket Gallery, Edinburgh

Barriers

There may be many reasons why the young people you're hoping to engage have never stepped foot in your gallery before or are not returning as independent visitors.

What young people say about their experience of museums and galleries:

- 'They make you nervous, the other people there… watching your every move'
- 'They are boring, exhibitions seem unapproachable and protective'
- Past experiences were not positive, especially enforced school visits with worksheets
- No age-appropriate activities for young people
- 'Galleries are uninviting… boxed off… segregated'
- 'The "approachable" staff don't look approachable'
- 'There is a stigma attached to them, which puts people off, kind of highbrow'
- 'Really better than I expected'
- 'It's actually quite interesting once you get in there'
- 'A bit formal and repetitive'
- 'I wouldn't choose to go to a museum or gallery for a day out'[1]

You need to discover what the potential barriers are between your organisation and young people. Go and find out by consulting with your colleagues and young people in your community. If you don't have an existing relationship with young people or want to conduct a wider consultation try:

- Local youth magazines
- Go into your local youth club or school
- Local youth radio stations
- Access a local youth websites forum
- Contact local youth organisations many of whom will have access to youth forums, youth councils, consultation groups and websites. There will be a team dedicated to this in your local Youth Service, usually called the Engagement or Participation Team.
- Your local Children and Young People's Plan by the Children's Services department in the local authority will include feedback from young people about what they want to do locally
- Your local Council for Voluntary Services

[1] Quotes from *Testing the Water: Young People and Museums*, and consultation with Nottingham Youth Theatre

" There is no doubt that galleries and museums are a fantastic resource for all of the community not just young people. However, there is a 'way of being' in a gallery that is not necessarily a social skill that all of us have acquired or are comfortable with. The silence, the white walls, the cameras, the climate controls and the gallery assistants who keep you under constant observation as if you intend to break something anyway. Often the very nature of a gallery space makes young people feel uncomfortable. **"**

Clare Mitchell, Regional Youth Officer, Government Office West Midlands

'Way In Way Out', Angel Row Gallery, 2004

Barriers exercise

envision carried out an exercise with
gallery educators and asked them to
come up with barriers they felt their
organisations had which inhibited
youth-friendly practice.

Prioritise what
galleries can deliver

facilities / resources not
equipped to meet
their needs

fear of giving
up control

Re assess
target Audience &
their expectations

not knowing
how to handle
young people

highlight gallery's
short comings

Additional request /
demand on FOH

talk to them –
take risks

fear of
unknown

Don't want them
to be disappointed

not target
customer

big job!

Sustained

Demonisation of
young people

Accidents

Young people
to meet
staff ; talk
about the
value of
art

Security of
artworks

Galleries to
take risks

Diversity of needs
& choices

Theft
defacement

Disturbance to
other visitors

Challenging behaviour
to staff /users

Allocate time
for kids / families

Status quo

Positive
representation of
young people within
the gallery environment

disadvantaged
/
bringing in
other agendas
+ expertise

Creative programming
with cross generational
shared experiences.

`constant

74

Engaging young people

Recruitment

Involving young people in active participation is all about building personal relationships with individuals and you'll need to think about working with small groups, probably a maximum of 10–12 young people, maybe less. Even with smaller numbers, recruitment can take time. Ideally meet young people on their own turf before any activity begins and before you work with them at the gallery, so that their interests and support needs can input into the planning.

Researching the artists and artworks before visiting the gallery can help to create a sense of expectation and anticipation, strengthen the context of a gallery visit and ultimately engage more young people.

❝Arc (alternative education organisation) participants invited us to lunch, which they made themselves, where we presented the project and completed baseline evaluation. Part of this session was spent compiling a skills audit and establishing the participants' interests and previous experience. This allowed us to tailor the sessions to meet real need and helped us to identify what activities might be challenging or appealing. ❞

Alice Walton, Education Co-ordinator, Living Art project, Metropole Gallery, Folkestone

Case study:

Wordz Out

Nottingham Castle Museum and Art Gallery organised a project that explored the barriers and issues young African Caribbean people experience living in Nottingham, culminating in a series of seven films revealing the diversity of black experience, achievement and talent in the city. The project brought together a committed core team of 11 young black people recruited individually by the outreach officer and staff team. This was achieved using a variety of traditional and innovative methods including flyers, employing a community ambassador and an evening recruitment music event at the Castle.

❝ [It was my] first museum experience. I thought museums were just photos and paintings… yes it's given me a different idea of what museums can offer. ❞

Participant, Wordz Out, Nottingham Castle Museum and Art Gallery

Broadly speaking young people are more likely to get involved in your activity if they have a sense of ownership in its process – that you are planning an activity with rather than for them. Design your work to allow young people to take responsibility for specific areas. Initially this may be a quite small role, developing into something larger with time. envision projects worked well where participants were able to input into the planning times, locations, dates, content and future facilitators.

Having said that some young people may not want to commit to planning and just want to turn up – as individuals you need to cater for a variety of interests, abilities and commitment, but you'll need to find this out first.

If physically meeting up with the young people prior to the workshop just can't happen try:

- Introducing the project and asking some questions via a phone call or, if appropriate, a referral form or written questionnaire
- A youth partner staff member could facilitate a consultation with the group for you
- If you can't ask the young people directly then try talking to staff, parents or carers who know them

At the very least you'll need to know if any of the young people have any access needs some time in advance to make sure you can support them to participate fully.

❝Young people pointed to the need for galleries to vigorously advertise their youth activities in local schools and perhaps also in youth clubs and sports centres, and to make direct contacts with art teachers. Schools are familiar with giving out information about clubs and activities and would gladly include information on a gallery project. They said that direct contact with art teachers was particularly important so that teachers could encourage nervous young people to take part.❞

Dr Jacqueline Watson, Enquire East: Learning for Empowerment, engage, 2007

Ideas for recruiting and engaging young people

- Advertise through partner organisations who work with young people
- Produce flyers, which can be photocopied – they don't need to be expensive
- Use free distribution networks such as your local authority mailshots for the youth service and schools
- Youth websites
- Local radio
- Local youth magazines
- PR on the street – link up with detached youth workers
- Use creative PR or 'happenings' to publicise events with processional sculptures, placards, banners etc
- Community ambassadors – engage a key youth worker, artist or community leader who's well respected by young people to be an advocate for your project
- Use young people as ambassadors
- Host taster sessions prior to the start of projects so young people can sample activity before committing
- Word of mouth: perhaps the most important and successful strategy

Communication

Agree with young people how you will contact them throughout the project. Some envision projects found texting a successful way to communicate reminders of forthcoming sessions and keeping young people informed of changes. If this proves a good idea, invest in a mobile phone for the project (never use your personal phone).

Transport

How are the young people going to get to your venue? Some people might be quite capable and motivated to get public transport – others might need a bit more support. Will you or partners be providing taxis, minibuses or reimbursing bus fares? If working in rural areas where the travel time to the venue is considerable, acknowledge this. Maybe you or the artist could travel with the young people, providing informal contact time and use this journey to develop creative activity as part your project.

Creating a welcoming environment

You may feel that you're limited by the sterile 'white box' gallery space or the 'intimidating' entrance hall, but there are small things you can do to make the space more welcoming to young people:

• Have the door open (obvious, but important)
• Ensure someone is there to meet and welcome the group at the door
• Encourage front of house staff – including caretakers and security staff – to be welcoming and friendly
• Bring a CD player
• Change the lighting
• Provide tea and/or juice and toast and encourage young people to make this independently for themselves and for each other
• Find ways that young people can make their own mark on the space
• Create a chill out or time-out space with cushions and beanbags
• Use the gallery café (if you have one) as a time-out/discussion space, which can encourage the young people to mix with other gallery visitors and feel comfortable about returning there on other occasions as a place to go
• Approach the project as a team with both staff and young people working together on an equal footing
• Use ice breakers and team building activities involving all the staff

Some of this will depend somewhat on whether you're working with young people in the gallery space when it's open for public access; this is something to bear in mind when you're planning. If you're proposing to do some really hands-on activity consider whether an alternative, neutral space, with few distractions, can be used. However be aware that part of your focus should be on the young people developing a relationship with and sense of ownership of the gallery space too.

❝Concern was raised in the planning stage about the workshop sessions being in the main gallery space while it was open to the general public but this did not worry the young people themselves. On the contrary, working with artists and Q Arts staff in a public forum appeared to raise their sense of legitimacy in occupying the gallery space.❞

Amanda McLaren, Programme Officer (Participation and Learning), Q Arts

Providing some kind of refreshments is especially important, whatever time of day you're running your activity. If you're planning an all day event you will need to provide a lunch – but even if you're organising a two-hour evening session it's good to provide something simple to eat and drink. Some young people might not have eaten a great deal before they arrive at the gallery. But do avoid fizzy drinks, too much caffeine and sugary food for obvious reasons! You will need to be aware of allergies though.

If you can make the refreshment area slightly separate from the workshop area it gives a secondary space for people to use if they need a break.

Flexibility

A flexible approach to facilitating the activity is absolutely crucial. Be aware that many young people will have had limited experience of galleries and education spaces beyond their school environment – you'll need to give them enough information and experience to make informed opinions. It's obviously difficult to make an informed decision about whether you like contemporary sculpture if you've never experienced it before, so as much as possible allow for the project to develop and grow with the young people's interests, ideas and commitment. Most funders will positively encourage young people's decision-making to influence the activity. See Getting started for more on fundraising for projects.

You'll still need initial activity to be structured. Start working with an activity that most of the group will be familiar and comfortable with (perhaps from a school experience) to let them find their feet with you and the building. Give them some confidence before offering a range of opportunities and choices.

Once you've got to know more about who you are working with, implement that knowledge into your planning.

Timing

Timing will be somewhat determined by when you can get access to the gallery but you also need take into consideration young people's other commitments and issues, for example: medication, lie-ins at the weekend, exam times, travel times, rush hour traffic, other big events in your local area and holidays. If you're working with young people in full-time education are school holidays a good or bad time to programme workshops? You can programme longer blocks of daytime sessions but this has pros and cons:

Pros
- Relationships and a sense of teamwork build more quickly
- You can create a more intense experience
- It's easier to manage resources
- You can take over a space for the period of the project (leaving out resources so that there is no tidying up or setting up time)

Cons
- Inconsistency of participants and staff; some young people, youth partner staff and gallery staff may have booked holidays
- It will require lots of energy and commitment from you and the young people
- Young people feel they're entitled to time-out from learning
- Young people get distracted by what their peers not involved in the project are up to

City Art's Apt youth project have developed a successful approach, planning new projects in term time, meeting once a week in the early evening to build confidence and interest and to iron out any issues. During this time they discuss with participants times and days for a more intense block of activity for the approaching holiday period.

Where possible leave some flexibility in your budget to adapt your plans to respond to young people's interests and commitments. You will also need to put aside specific funds for support costs which you'll be able allocate once you've talked to your partners and young people to find out their access needs. The following list gives some guidance on what to think about when planning your budget:

- Access needs: interpreters, personal assistants, child care or specific transport costs
- Transport: taxi, bus and train fares, minibus
- Refreshments
- Artists' fees
- Materials
- Training: to address any skills or awareness gaps for yourself and colleagues
- Partnership development events: opportunities to share skills and build the partnership
- Accreditation
- Enhanced Criminal Record Board (CRB) checks for all staff (including volunteers) who are in direct contact with young people
- Support workers: if employing on an hourly rate, remember to factor in time for planning, setting up and packing away, feedback before and after the sessions, and evaluation meetings etc
- Volunteers: transport, refreshments and CRB checks
- Marketing
- Exhibition costs
- Celebratory event including invites and refreshments
- Contingency (at least 20% for flexibility)

Funders may want to see what your organisation is contributing to the project. So include venue hire, your time and other colleagues involved including your line manager's time. See Getting started for more guidance on fundraising.

Budgeting

Taking risks and managing expectations

Part of the benefits of working with a group of young people is about them informing our practice with their fresh and exciting ideas. It's about opening our doors and being open to the change that brings. Taking risks in the envision projects generally paid off. It demonstrated a commitment to and trust in the young people which was reciprocated. It challenged traditional ideas of what a gallery space should and could be.

If a project doesn't meet your expectations, don't give up hope and don't be afraid to risk doing something again, even if it went wrong before. If you know you managed the project to the best of your ability and have evaluated properly, it will provide a valuable learning experience and give you practical knowledge about how you plan in the future.

Managing Expectations

In creating a youth-friendly gallery with young people be honest with yourself, your colleagues and young people about what you can realistically offer. Share your motivations, your restrictions and the potential of this work. Be honest about how much time and commitment this work needs, the activity may initially appear resource heavy for quite limited outcomes but if it is delivered well the investment should lead to bigger and better things.

Involve young people in the evaluation process rather than imposing it upon them – let them know why you're doing it – make it a shared process. They could have some ideas about how they'd like to feedback comments to you. See Wrapping up and Resources to get more advice on evaluation methods.

Relationship building can take time. If you want young people to offer their honest opinions it's vital to generate trust so that young people feel motivated and open about sharing their thoughts with you. Let them know what will happen to their comments, that their ideas may not be actioned immediately and that decisions may take time and need to be brokered. Acknowledge the learning you and your organisation have gained from the young people and be honest about any mistakes.

Is the programme time-limited because of funding? Can the young people help fundraise to continue and develop the project? If so how long will it take for funding decisions to be made? See Getting started for more advice on fundraising.

" Empower the teens but be prepared for what happens. There is a fine line between too much freedom and too much structure. The first year of the [young people's] Council, we made the mistake of telling the teens they could do what they wanted without the caveat of 'within the context and bounds of working in a public institution'. Some lengthy and powerful discussions about issues of censorship followed. The end result: both adults and teens realised that 'empowerment' means negotiation, dialogue and sometimes compromise. **"**

Walker Art Center, Minneapolis,
Teen Program's How-To Kit, 1999

Maximising outcomes

Where appropriate, make the most of opportunities to showcase the project – work as a group to publicise your achievements to local young people, your organisation, the community, funders and policy makers. Link up with websites, young people's magazines, community newspapers, radio and events.

As well as adding to a sense of achievement, sharing your project with a wider audience will also increase both the young people's and the gallery's profile locally and help to make the case for continuing the work. Good documentation makes a great impact and is a vital tool for communicating the value of your project. See Wrapping up for more ideas on promoting your project to others.

Sharing information: confidentiality and marketing

It is essential that you have written consent for any photographs/images taken of the young people from the participants and their parents or carers. Use images only for the purposes you specifically agree with the young people. In the case of young people in residential care, consent may not be possible to obtain. You can still document a project but only use photographs that do not identify individuals, such as images of hands and backs of heads. For an example of a photo consent form see the envision toolkit, Templates and Guidelines section at www.en-vision.org.uk

When working with specific groups be respectful about how you name and market projects. Ask the young people how they want to be represented in publicity. Young people do not often identify with or are proud of the labels they are given. Remember that information/publicity often has a long circulation so do not label young people in a way that they may regret in years to come if not right now.

Have a written policy and agreement about the publicity of the project that you share with all partners and your organisation's marketing colleagues – they may not have the same approach as you and you could find that young people are represented in a way that they would not have chosen.

Creating a safe environment

When working with or providing services for young people you will need to understand the responsibilities that you, your colleagues and your organisation are taking on. Have a written policy and set of procedures in place. There are some very good resources and training available to help you do this. See Resources for details.

Although we are keen to celebrate young people and focus on the positives of engaging with them, we also don't want to ignore the fact that sometimes young people can present unexpected and/or disruptive behaviour.

Are you working with young people who are engaging on a voluntary basis (through a youth project for example) or are they attending as part of their education or because of a court order? This can greatly affect the way young people view the project, at least initially, and this is something you need to be aware of.

When working with excluded and vulnerable groups, young people's lives may be very chaotic, frustrating and stressful. They may see your project as a bit of a refuge and you may be offering some really valuable time and space away from their daily problems. There is also the possibility that some of those frustrations and tensions may lead to behaviour which is challenging and you and the staff involved in the project – including front of house – will need to have in place a practical strategy for dealing with this.

Be prepared

In your planning you will need to address:

- How many staff are needed to support the sessions?
- Are partner organisation's staff going to be present to support the project?
- Who has 'duty of care' for the young people?
- Who will obtain parental consent for the young people to attend the project?
- Does your partner organisation work using specific ground rules for their group and will they be the same rules for this project?
- Do partners, and possibly parents, intend to use attendance at the project in their rewards and sanctions for young people? If so you'll need to persuade them against this.
- Who will you ask for relevant personal details about individual young people and how will you use this information?

Risk assessment

It's vital to carry out a risk assessment for your activity with young people, identifying:

- Hazards
- Who or what is at risk
- The extent of the risk
- Measures you can put in place to minimise risk
- What action needs to be taken by whom and by when to put these measures in place

This can be used in your planning meeting with the project staff and give you, your colleagues and any project partners more confidence that you've thought everything through and prepared things to the best of your ability.

For an example of a Risk Assessment Form see the envision toolkit, Templates and Guidance section at www.en-vision.org.uk

Managing a project team

In managing your project team you will need to consider:

- Who will take overall responsibility for the project?
- What are the roles and responsibilities of everyone involved in the project?
- How will new responsibilities fit in with existing ones?
- How will you communicate with all parties involved in the project?
- How will progress will be monitored and reviewed?
- How will you provide practical and administrative support for those involved in the project?

To deliver your project you may find yourself working with a small team of artists, partner staff, gallery colleagues, volunteers, young people and support staff and you'll need to find ways of managing everyone's role. Get everyone involved in the planning and make sure all staff are kept informed, clear about their roles and responsibilities, and able to share their knowledge and advice.

Jargon Buster

Duty of care is seen in the eyes of the law as 'a duty to act as a careful parent would' by providing adequate supervision for the young people in your care.

This will depend upon things such as age, the maturity of the young people, the type of activity and numbers involved, which should be discussed in relation to a risk assessment for the project.

If you cause injury or loss because you were not working in a careful way, you could be held accountable by civil law for negligence. If a young person causes loss or damage to someone else or their property whilst under your supervision, you could also be liable.

If you are taking on duty of care for a young person you also need to be aware of their personal details and how you use this information. Some of this information will be confidential and you will need to make professional judgements about sharing information with colleagues on a need-to-know basis. For example, you might need to let project staff know that 'Sarah' is uncomfortable about working with male staff members, but not disclose details of what has happened in her life that has led to this.

Support Workers

The role of a support worker is invaluable in providing pastoral support and duty of care expertise. It's important to maintain the same support staff throughout the project. They will have a deeper understanding of the aims, objectives and outcomes and feel a greater sense of investment in the project. This will help in developing the relationship between the staff team and the participants and crucially provide better, more consistent support for the young people. If that person is from a new youth partner then this could also provide a valuable learning experience for them in what galleries can offer young people and make them a champion for this work within their organisation.

For an example of a support worker's roles and responsibilities see the envision toolkit, Templates and Guidelines section at www.en-vision.org.uk

Group agreement

In your first session with young people at the gallery it's important to discuss the practicalities of working in the building. It's a good idea to draw up a group agreement together about the way in which you all want to work as a team

(for example, respect for each other, respect for the venue, guidance on when you can have cigarette breaks or time-outs) which everyone can to sign up to. Encourage participants and front of house staff to contribute to this and create the opportunity for everyone to discuss codes of conduct in the space and the front of house staff's role. Some envision projects made this a creative ice breaker exercise.

Pin the signed group agreement to the wall at every session and if any situations do arise you can refer back to the agreement as a reminder about what the ground rules for participation are.

If you need to intervene:

- Keep calm. By maintaining control you can help the young person to set limits for his or her behaviour
- Let other staff know about any concerns or developing situations as soon as possible, and call for support
- Treat young people as individuals. Even with prior knowledge of an individual's backgrounds be diplomatic: listen and respect a young person's viewpoint of the situation before making assumptions
- Debrief with the staff team after every session. Note any issues and discuss as a team how you will manage this at the next session and how this will impact on your planning for the rest of the project

Professional boundaries

As a gallery educator your relationship with young people will not be easily recognised as that of a 'teacher' or 'social worker' and may be regarded more as a friendly adult. This may have great benefits, particularly for young people who have had a troubled family background or a negative experience of formal education. You could become a much needed positive role model and in some instances the young person's first positive relationship with an adult.

However with this comes responsibility. It is therefore very important to behave in ways that can't be misinterpreted and to keep to a professional code of conduct at all times.

Be clear about boundaries between personal and professional life and be prepared for the tensions that may arise between developing a caring, supportive relationship with young people and the need to maintain professional boundaries.

When there are no other support staff from partner organisations present, then you and your organisation will legally have 'duty of care'.

Some recommendations:

- Avoid situations when there is only one adult present with young people
- Be aware of the potential for abuse from other young people
- Work closely with partner agencies that know the young people to identify and reduce potential risk
- Ensure that all workers who have regular contact with young people receive child protection training in order to raise levels of awareness to enable them to deal with situations effectively and to protect everyone involved
- Ensure you have an incident reporting procedure in place and staff and volunteers are aware of it

Avoiding vulnerable situations

Successful working with young people is built on relationships of trust. Young people need to trust that we will not talk about them with other people or share personal information. However if a young person discloses information about abuse or activity that is putting them at risk, then it is our professional obligation to share this with the local Children's Social Care Team, for investigation.

All staff should take particular care not to develop close personal or sexual relationships with the young people they are working with – it's exploitative and could be illegal.

look with your eyes Not with your hands!

'LivingArt', Metropole Gallery, 2007

Some strategies:

- Avoid being on your own with a young person behind a closed door
- Do not invite a young person to your home or visit them at their home
- Avoid touching young people unless it's part of your directed role
- Avoid giving young people lifts in your car
- Do not accept gifts

If you have reasons to believe a young person has developed a crush on you inform your line manager and partner staff at the earliest opportunity, and have your concerns noted.

Staff behaviour

It's the staff's role to model appropriate behaviour and set a clear benchmark of what is acceptable, this includes: providing a positive and encouraging atmosphere, showing how an adult can be anti-oppressive and non-exploitative but still caring, assertive and willing to join in the fun. This promotes a culture that ensures everyone is listened to and respected as individuals.

Emergencies

Ensure you have signed parental consent forms for the young people attending with emergency contact numbers. Inform the young person's parent or carer, your manager and any partner organisation staff at the earliest opportunity if an emergency arises.

Child protection

Issues of child protection apply to working with all young people and some basic rules of good practice apply:

- If you do not already have one, instigate an organisational Child Protection Policy
- Ensure that all staff in contact with young people have a current Criminal Records Bureau (CRB) disclosure certificate. Disclosures can take weeks to be processed and returned; something to be aware of in your planning
- CRB checks can only be submitted through registered or 'umbrella' organisations

See the CRB website for more information and for details of local registered organisations at www.crb.gov.uk/. Try your local Safeguarding Children Board for information about training and help with writing a Child Protection Policy. And see Resources for more information on Child Protection.

" We have had some behavioural problems and on one occasion this presented a risk to the exhibition, which was very worrying and made us question the viability of working in such close proximity to the work in a small gallery. We transferred to a project workspace in conjunction with visiting the gallery, which worked better. This afforded us some peace of mind and gave the young people space to spread them selves out. It was also recognising that the young people were extremely lively, full of energy and curiosity and they helped us to work with it rather than having to place constant restrictions.**"**

Mandy Roberts, artist and Co-ordinator on the NR5 into Outpost project

However skilled an artist may be, their attitude and understanding of engaging young people is what will help decide who you work with.

Often the most talented and intelligent artists are not the best teachers – you need someone who is able to connect with young people and translate ideas and skills.

Finding an artist you trust will be a big relief and could be the key to your project's success. However working with the same artist again and again will restrict the artforms you introduce to young people. To avoid this you'll have to take some risks in working with new people. To limit these risks ask around, get recommendations, get references and involve young people in the recruitment process.

To give less established artists the opportunity to gain experience and an opportunity for you to see them interact with young people, you could offer shadowing or volunteering opportunities.

Involving young people in recruitment

In many instances young people will know better than gallery staff what sort of artist they and their peers might want to work with.

Some ideas:

- Young people could meet and greet candidates as they arrive for an interview and show them round the building
- One or two young people could help in shortlisting and interviewing – you'll need to brief the young people first about their role
- Ask the artists to facilitate a short exercise with the young people as part of the interview

The role of the artist

The role of the artist might vary from project to project with a different emphasis on different roles. You might choose someone who's more of a youth specialist than an artist. To create more of a direct link to the gallery, and/or due to limited resources, you might be the facilitator yourself.

Using professional artists and technicians can add value, impact and credibility to the project. You might decide to employ someone for a very specific purpose but usually an artist will be asked to meet a number of the following roles:

- As facilitator: introducing artforms and new skills, encouraging and supporting young people's own creativity
- As a creative consultant
- As a role model and inspiration for a creative career
- As collaborator on a specific piece of work
- As motivator, trainer, teacher, mentor, adviser

There are also some fantastic web-based resources to use with young people to explore the world of contemporary artists and people working in the creative industries. Some of these include: DCMS Culture Online website with links to projects and interactive sites including ArtisanCam, a video and interactive resource for young people including interviews from artists, curators and gallery technicians, at www.cultureonline.gov.uk. AccessArt, a website made with young people for young people called Teenage Creativity and the Immersive Learning Space, which is a great site to explore the creative processes of different artists, dancers, architects and graphic designers, at www.accessart.org.uk

Contracts

To ensure a professional working relationship, all work should be contracted properly with a written and signed agreement which considers dates, times, payment details, insurance, the roles and responsibilities of the gallery, support staff and artist, copyright, resources and what happens in the event of cancellation. Once you have a template it won't take much time to maintain this important part of administration. For an example see envision toolkit Templates and Guidelines section at www.en-vision.org.uk

Fees

There are various guidelines on rates of pay for freelance artists. Artquest's website currently suggests: 'Self-employed artists (when taking on short-term contracts of between one and five days and with experience of their field) should be offered a daily rate set of around £175–£300 per day. This rate decreases when the contract stretches beyond a working week up to twenty-one days. Artists should work for no less than £20 hour; artists in London should charge around 7.5% on top of this for London Market Allowance.'

Briefing notes

It's also important to have a thorough set of best practice guidelines for freelancers you employ to work with young people. These should include a job description, the aims and objectives of the project, reference to your child protection policy, CRB checks, professional boundaries and expected codes of conduct.

Issues

To really commit to sustainable youth-friendly practice be aware that young people's relationships need to develop not just with a freelance artist or partner staff but also with the gallery, its space and its staff. So make sure you have a presence within the activity – maybe you'll be leading it. Introduce the front of house staff – give them a role and get them involved. Young people are more likely to make independent return visits if they make a relationship with someone who will be there to welcome them when they come back.

Youth-friendly practice is about organisational change. The idea is not just about creating a youth-friendly education policy but an accessible youth-friendly space which is embraced and has impact across the whole organisation: on programming, on front of house, on marketing, on management – on every aspect of the venue. See Wrapping up for more discussion about organisational change.

Where to look for artists

Websites:

The Ann Peaker Centre has a database of artists and organisations working with the criminal justice system. Go to www.apcentre.org.uk

Aliss includes a database of artists working in participatory arts in the West Midlands. Go to www.aliss.org.uk

The Voluntary Arts Network includes a national directory of artists. Go to www.voluntaryarts.org

❝ It was felt that this shift in opinion or [increased] level of involvement from the young people was nurtured by having a connection with people at the gallery… rather than any real shift in the beliefs they had before. In other words, they now come to the gallery and are interested because they know people here and want to continue that relationship rather than because they think the art is really good. Inevitably they see and are exposed to contemporary art on their visits so slowly their opinions may shift we hope. ❞

Victoria Mayes, Offsite and Outreach Education Co-ordinator, Milton Keynes Gallery

Organisations:

Your regional Arts Council email groups

www.educatorlocator.org

Local arts organisations

Your local authority Arts Development Officer

Advertise:

Artsjobs is Arts Council England's free daily email for creative opportunities

engage's weekly careers e-bulletin (free to members)

ENYAN (English National Youth Arts Network) website and regional groups www.enyan.co.uk

a-n Artists' Newsletter magazine

Local press

Notice boards in studios, galleries and arts centres

'NR5 into Outpost', Outpost Gallery and Fruitful Arts, 2007

Case study:

Living Art

The Metropole Gallery worked in partnership with Arc 25 and Pathways (both alternative curriculum providers) to introduce young people to creative ways of expression whilst exploring unfamiliar experiences.

The project was developed and led by artists, Alice Walton, Abi Gilchrist and Natasha Kidd whose creative approach meant that every element of the project became a creative experience and opportunity for participants to make or think in a creative way, helping develop self expression and confidence.

"We attempted to take a quirky approach to the mundane activities that featured throughout the project, regardless of the setting, such as travelling, having tea or stopping for lunch. We introduced playful activities that challenged the group's expectations of an arts based project, which further served to change preconceived attitudes about certain places, people or modes of behaviour."

Alice Walton, freelance Education Co-ordinator, Metropole Gallery, Folkestone

The project was clearly valued by the young people:

❝It was really good and I liked going to London for the day and creating loads of things I had never done before and making our own cups was really cool and I really I iked going to Margate but it is so crap because it has to end! It was great!❞

Young person, Living Art, project, Metropole Gallery, Folkestone

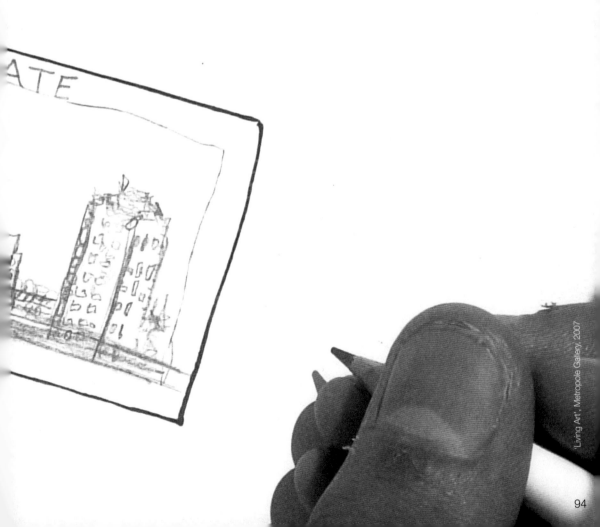

'Living Art', Metropole Gallery, 2007

Working with volunteers

Volunteering should also be recognised as an important two-way relationship between the organisation and the individual. Many projects rely on volunteers; their skills and assistance can bring valuable support to a project, whilst providing them with valuable experience and an opportunity to contribute to their community.

When employing a volunteer ask for references and use an application form to formalise the arrangement and to clarify expectations of the volunteer and the organisation. Involve volunteers in team planning and training and let them know their contribution is valued.

Volunteering provides an opportunity for artists and youth workers to gain experience to develop their careers and it can also provide a significant opportunity for young people to progress from participant to a staff team member. This can offer young people fantastic learning opportunities, new responsibilities and key transferable work skills, whilst the gallery gains a valuable asset in a peer support worker. Participants are more likely to engage with a project if they can see other young people committed and supportive of the activity. If working with young volunteers you may want to consider some form of 'reward' for their time, for example gift vouchers, accreditation or a good reference.

Case study:

Excelerate

198 Gallery in London developed opportunities for a group of young people outside of formal education who were attending 198's digital media education programme. Excelerate opened up 198's adult volunteering programme to the younger group and gave the young people valuable work based learning opportunities.

" Using artists and their work to inspire and motivate young people is well established, but Excelerate aimed to give young people more responsibility and for the artistic programme to benefit from their ideas and energy. The gallery has a long history of working with volunteers but this project provided the opportunity for a different kind of young person to get involved in the exhibitions. **"**

Lucy Davies, Director, 198 Gallery, London

Participants' involvement varied between two days and two weeks depending on their availability, the area of work and their level of commitment. Young people worked on exhibition installation, curatorial consultancy, PR, marketing and event management, promotional material design, photographic documentation and web page design.

" We have seen that we can have a changing pool of talent and enthusiasm that can contribute to the programme and extend the central role of volunteers to the organisation. It also gives young people the 'real' experiences they want to help them move forward with their careers and shows that their contribution is valued and recognised. **"**

Lucy Davies, Director, 198 Gallery, London

'Wordzout', Nottingham Castle
Museum and Art Gallery, 2005

Notes

Wrapping up

Jo Wheeler and Francois Matarasso

In this section the handbook offers guidance on evaluating your project and how to use your learning to influence organisational change and inform and extend your future work with young people. It links closely with the planning and learning guidance in Getting Started.

Evaluation methods

Evaluation depends on being able to collect data about what has happened, within the framework of the aim, objectives and indicators set out at the start. Much of that data will be concerned with observing change of various kinds:

- Changes in attitudes, behaviour or expectations among those involved: staff and partners as much as the young people themselves
- Changes between plans and delivery
- Changes in gallery use, programme or policy

In some larger or more ambitious projects, it may be useful to record key indicators at the outset and at the end of a project. So, for example, there may be an induction process involving an interview or asking new participants to complete a self-assessment questionnaire about their experience and view of art.

Gathering information

There are lots of ways of gathering information. In fact, the main problem is not collecting it but doing it well, consistently and reliably. It's easy to collect data, but much harder to collect good data. Many projects focus on quantity of information rather than quality. They end up with a tangle of not very good material, when it would have been perfectly sufficient just to keep track of three or four key indicators, such as attendance and changes in attitude.

There are different ways of talking to people about their experience of your work. You can talk to people directly, individually or in groups, you can ask them to complete a questionnaire or you can try some less structured methods such as setting up a video booth or a blog on which people can record and discuss their views. The choice will be dictated by the circumstances, the needs of the evaluation and the values of your organisation.

Keep evaluation in proportion: it's not the purpose of the project, just a way of doing the project better. It should help you think about your practice critically, understand your work better and share knowledge with your key partners.

Quantitative data

There's lots of basic factual, ie quantitative, information about a project that can be immensely valuable. The most obvious things are demographics, ie information about the participants, for example age, gender and ethnicity, and attendance records, but you may find that partners such as education or youth services keep their own records of young people's progress that are helpful to you in tracking change.

Apart from your own or other people's record keeping, you can collect data through questionnaires. This need not only be factual data, such as a respondent's age or whether they have visited the gallery before, questionnaires can also be used to quantify qualitative data, such as people's opinions.

Using questionnaires

Questionnaires have some important advantages:

- They can be anonymous and may encourage some people to be more open
- They take much less staff time than interviews and the results are recorded in written form
- It's possible to get the responses of a much larger group of people, including people who may live some distance away
- They can produce quantitative data and represent qualitative data, such as people's feelings, in quantitative form

Of course, questionnaires do present problems:

- People need a certain level of literacy (usually in English, although questionnaires can be prepared in other languages) and confidence in writing
- There's the danger that people who complete questionnaires are, to some extent, self-selecting and consequently unrepresentative

These problems can be reduced by using the questionnaire as the basis for a guided discussion or an interview so that people's responses are recorded for them by the discussion leader or interviewer.

Trying things out

When you have designed a questionnaire, try it out with someone first – not one of the participants – to check for:

- Intelligibility: are you asking people clear questions?
- Comprehension: can the questions be understood in more than one way?
- Meaningfulness: do they get useful responses?
- Omissions: do important issues arise which aren't covered?

And in doing all that, don't neglect the human aspects:

- How long does it take to complete the questionnaire?
- How do people respond to the questions?
- What information do they need to be given in order to answer the questions?

Use this experience to make changes and prepare for using the questionnaire at the end of the project.

There are some key questions to ask yourself about how you will use the questionnaire:

How will you prepare the young people for the exercise, for example in explaining why you need it, what you will do with the answers and the importance of their honesty in answering?

Will you ask participants to fill in the questionnaire themselves or use it as the framework for an interview?

Will you ask them all to do it at the same time (if you decide that they should write it themselves)?

Will they complete it on site or take it away?

What environments or situations are likely to be most productive if it's done as a series of individual interviews?

Case study:

X-Panel (Handover)

Spacex Gallery devised the 'swimming pool' exercise as part of the evaluation for their youth-led programming project, to track change in the young people's involvement. Near the beginning of the project participants and staff were asked to imagine the gallery floor space as a swimming pool. They were asked to place themselves somewhere in the pool and to say what they were doing and how they felt about it. This provided a good starting point for discussion about the gallery, the project and the young people's response to it.

❝I am on the edge because I don't know what I am doing here. ❞

Young person

Over the course of the project the young people organised an exhibition, several events and activities. Just before the final event – a gig by a local band in the gallery space – the exercise was repeated and the swimming pool looked very different: everyone was in the deep end.

The Swimming Pool Exercise:
Project participants were asked to imagine that the gallery were a swimming pool. They were then asked to tell everyone what they were doing in the swimming pool and how they felt about it. This gave everyone the opportunity to express their doubts about the project and feelings of involvement in the gallery without talking about it in concrete terms. Participants said things like 'I am on the edge because I don't know what I am doing here' and 'I am in the shallow end but want to get to the deep end.' This articulated their feelings about the gallery and provided a starting point for discussion about the gallery environment.

One the very last day of the project, just before the music event they had organised the group repeated the exercise. This time the swimming pool looked very different: everyone was in the pool's deep end. There was still a lot to be done for that evening's event, so there was not much discussion about how they felt in the deep end but it was evident from their decisive position that they felt, at the least, involved in the gallery.

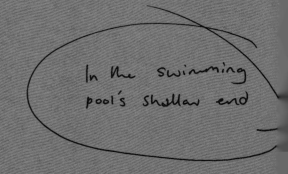

In the swimming pool's shallow end

In the pool but not
swimming confidently

Watching from
the edge

Project facilitator
in the middle of
the pool facing
the shallow end

es in the water
 edge of the deep
d deciding whether
 jump in

Who should complete the questionnaire?

It's important that you get responses from everyone who has been involved in the project. If people take away the questionnaires, make sure that you get them back. You might like to ask any adults, such as teachers or youth workers, who've accompanied the young people to complete the questionnaire as well: this will give everyone confidence and demonstrate fairness.

Don't forget to think about how you might get answers from any of the people who have dropped out: can you visit their school or youth club to speak to them? Could they talk to you over the phone or answer some of the questions by email or text? It's likely they will be unwilling to do a full questionnaire but even getting a couple of answers from them – as well as asking why they dropped out – would be valuable.

Questionnaire checklist

- When, where and how will the questionnaires be administered?
- Will they be completed by respondents or through interviews?
- Will they be completed on site or will people take them away?
- How will they be collected and by whom?
- Do you understand every question?
- If any question is open to more than one interpretation, can you say what it means?
- Have you tested the questionnaire beforehand?

Qualitative data

In this context, qualitative data is used to mean information that is either not factual, such as the interpretation of a situation, or cannot be meaningfully compared, such as someone's enjoyment of an activity. Qualitative research methods – of which the most obvious are probably observation and talking to people – are also a good way of testing the information that comes from quantitative sources. Asking people about some of the things that seem to emerge from completed questionnaires is a good way of testing their and your understanding of both process and situation.

Observation

Observing what's happening is often underestimated because it's such an everyday thing to do, especially when running workshops, but an experienced educator or artist can learn a lot by watching participants and how they engage or interact. The value of observation is greatly enhanced if it is more conscious and methodical and if the results are recorded during or shortly after sessions. Criteria for observation – what you're looking for – can be developed from indicators, which helps structure this process. See Getting started for more about indicators.

❝ We attempted to build an evaluative element into every practical activity, placing an emphasis on the young people's views and ideas both in terms of making work and expressing their opinions. **❞**

Alice Walton, freelancer Education Co-ordinator, Living Art project, Metropole Gallery

Interviews and discussions

The most obvious way to find out what people think is to interview them: face-to-face, by phone or in a small group. You can follow a more or less structured agenda or a set of questions, though you should also offer people a chance to speak freely about whatever interests them.

Someone involved with the project or an independent person can do an interview; the responses you get may be different depending on your approach. People may be more or less open with someone they have been working with or whose art they have strong feelings about. But an outsider may find it hard to appreciate the subtleties of a particular situation or may not ask about aspects which only those closely involved know about.

Interviews and discussion groups raise the problem of how to record what people say. In some cases, it may only be possible or appropriate to listen to what is being said and make a note of it afterwards. In other situations written notes can be made as people talk or a sound or video recording made. While the latter is the most reliable, in some situations it may be intimidating or unwelcome; it also involves considerable time in listening back and transcribing recordings.

Creative methods

It is also worth saying something about creative methods of gathering information. Making the process of self-reflection part of the activity can be hugely rewarding and strengthen both the project and the evaluation. Many artists have their own ideas and ways of doing this and others may come out of the workshops themselves. Among the most common are:

- Use a big scrapbook as a project diary in which anybody can draw, write or paste things in. You can complete it together as a group activity or leave it open and available at every session
- Use games and art activities to get people to visualise and represent their feelings and experiences
- Put up a big sheet of paper to act as a comment or graffiti wall
- Set up a diary room or a blog
- Text people a single question after a session
- Ask some of the group to take responsibility for evaluation, to interview each other or to film and photograph activities. Some young people may be more willing to engage in the project in this way.

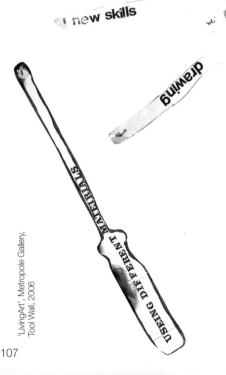

new skills

to be good

drawing

MATERIALS

USEING DIFFERENT

'LivingArt', Metropole Gallery, Tool Wall, 2006

❝ Throughout the research in all the projects, photographs and video was a vital part of recording evidence for the young people and the art educators/action researchers. Talking about the photographs and video footage and reflecting back on the experience of the projects was used as a natural and informal method for art educators to work with young people in evaluating the projects.**❞**

Dr Jacqueline Watson, Enquire East: Learning for Empowerment, engage, 2007

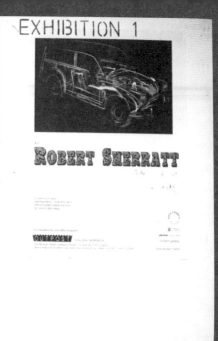

Tips on…
Creative evaluation methods

- Participatory techniques, for example; role play, drama, games, visualisation, drawings, diagrams, cartoons, sketches, maps
- Video booths, documentary-style videos providing commentary material and/or responses and recommendations
- Press conferences
- Roving reporters
- Expert panels or 'round table' discussion and Q&A
- Collective notice boards, storyboards, graffiti walls, comment boxes
- Young people's diaries, logs, scrapbooks (individual and group)

- Use of creative exercises such as colour, mood boards and images to help individuals articulate their thoughts
- Use of photographs and artefacts to trigger recollections and encourage analytical skills
- Young people presenting findings and responses at interim stages on a work in progress through presentations, reviews, display or multimedia product
- Document the data using note-taking alongside photography, audio or video recording

Note: it is important to date information so that you can chart progress and report on findings, even if the information is anonymous

❝Right at the end of the last session we projected questions onto the wall and the young people sprayed their answers very spontaneously using single words and symbols such as smiley faces and ticks. Questions included: Do you feel more confident in galleries? Did you learn enough art skills? Would you like more sessions in the workshop space? I asked them if there were questions I should have asked and they suggested: Did you like it? The answers were all very short but very positive.❞

Mandy Roberts, NR5 into Outpost project, Fruitful Arts

Both images: 'NR5 into Outpost', Outpost Gallery and Fruitful Arts, project diary, 2007

Tracking change: monitoring change in the gallery

Before the project starts, plan to monitor how many young people already visit the gallery, perhaps over the course of a week. What do you know about them? Are they in school parties, in family groups, with peers or on their own? What do they do when they're in the gallery? Are there areas or exhibits they respond to more than others?

Talk to gallery staff

All staff – front of house, invigilators, education team and curators – can have a big influence on how attractive and interesting a gallery is to young people. One way of tracking change is to talk to staff before and after a project to see how their own ideas and attitudes may have developed as a result. Questions might include:

- How well does the gallery cater for young people?
- What is it about this gallery that you think would interest young people?
- Do you have any concerns about increasing young people's use of the gallery space?
- How comfortable do you think young people find this gallery space?

At first, some staff may say that they don't have the experience to answer or that you should ask the young people themselves (you will). But what's important is what people think: if they believe that the gallery is open to young people but the young people say it isn't, they need to rethink their positions.

Young people

An obvious way of tracking change in participants is to ask them the same questions at the start and at the end of the project. That can be done using any of the techniques described above: interviews, questionnaires, video, online etc. Here is a list of questions that envision projects developed to ask young participants:

'NR5 into Outpost', Outpost Gallery and Fruitful Arts, 2007

109

Demographics: age, sex, ethnicity, disability

Education, training or employment situation

How did you hear about the project?

Have you visited this gallery before?

If yes, with who, when and in what context?

Which of these words best describes this place? Boring / exciting / friendly / welcoming / interesting / comfortable / intimidating / challenging / pointless / fun / not for me / confusing / scary

How do you rate your skills in the following areas: Working with others / Reliability / Creativity / Leadership / Communication

(on a scale of 1–5)

How comfortable do you feel with: Talking about ideas / Contemporary art / Thinking of new ideas / Being creative / Visiting new places (on a scale of 1–5)

What do you want to get out of this project?

Do you have any worries about coming to the gallery or taking part?

What kind of job or career are you interested in?

What is it about the gallery that you think might interest young people?

Whether it is appropriate or possible to use this approach will depend on the circumstances, of course. It will work better in more formal situations, where there is an induction process. In other situations, where building a relationship of trust has to be the first step, it would be wrong to start with this. Bear in mind also that the specific questions that you ask should always relate to the project's aim, objectives and indicators.

❝ Where art educators worked more closely with young people and over a longer period of time, it was possible to build up closer relationships between the adults and young people, so that adults were able to talk with the young people and learn from them through direct conversation. For the young people involved in these projects this seemed to be the best mechanism for evaluation and young people preferred to voice their opinions face-to-face. ❞

Dr Jacqueline Watson, Enquire East: Learning for Empowerment, engage, 2007

Partners

Many projects involve partners such as schools, exclusion units, the youth justice service and so on. They have their own aspirations for the project and will make their own judgements about its progress. They are an important source of information about the outcomes of the project for individual young people. For instance, they will normally have records of attendance at school or other provision. For young people involved with Youth Offending Teams, records of offending and fulfilment of court agreements during the project will also be important.

envision projects also used a range of questions to record the views of these partners. Questions included:

- Are there comparable activities you can benchmark this project against?
- Have you used arts as an intervention or activity before? If yes, in what context? With what success?
- What are your expectations from the partnership?
- Do you have any concerns or anxieties about the project?
- What is it about this gallery that you think would interest young people?

Ethics

It is important to be explicit with young people in the early stages about your project's aim, including any personal development benefits you anticipate and the purpose of the evaluation. In a one-to-one conversation young people are often upfront about their desire to build their confidence and make new friends. It also makes your job of assessing these outcomes and impacts a lot easier later on. For a larger project you may want to draw up an ethics statement to share with all interviewees, young people and staff. The following ethical principles should guide your approach to evaluation:

- Evaluation is a collective activity and the responsibility of all involved in the programme
- Confidentiality should be maintained throughout. Participants should not be named in the report. Images of participants are only used with their consent and the consent of their parents or carers

- Participants in the programme should be given the opportunity to comment on draft versions of the report for accuracy and fairness
- Young people are under no obligation to take part in the evaluation and are free to withdraw their comments at any time
- The final report should be available to all participants and partners

Reporting and learning

The purpose of all this planning and evaluation work is to learn and to share that learning with your partners and the young people you've been working with. Apart from anything else, people who provide you with information, who tell you their views and experiences, are entitled to hear what the results are of all those questions.

But reporting doesn't necessarily mean that you have to produce a weighty tome, detailing every aspect of the project, what you did and what everyone thought about it. Most people aren't that interested.

Projects that are genuinely innovative, which test new practice or ways of working, may merit a written report analysing their processes and making the findings available to other people working in the field. But in many cases, a short, clearly-written summary of a project's aim, its objectives, the extent to which they were met, and the key lessons that emerge, will be enough.

A post-project meeting of participants and partners to discuss the findings of an evaluation may actually be more valuable in the long run, since it encourages people to think about what happens next. That may involve everyone, or you may need to hold more than one meeting. These discussions should form the basis for your next project based on what you have learnt, demonstrating the cyclical nature of planning, delivery, evaluation and planning.

Organisational Change

The most successful envision projects were those where the whole organisation was committed to the idea of learning and change.

You might be fortunate in having a supportive management and colleagues that are right behind you and can see the clear benefits of working with and involving young people in decision-making in your organisation, or you may not.

This section is about recognising that some gallery educators may feel isolated and unsupported in their work with young people and the inevitable risk-taking this will involve. Involving young people in galleries is all about your whole organisation being open to change. If you don't have support behind you any change that takes place is going to be very limited. So how do you go about convincing your organisation that working with young people is worthwhile?

How do you persuade your organisation to embrace youth-friendly practice?

Hopefully this handbook has given you enough strong arguments to start persuading your colleagues that this kind of work is a good thing. The big ideas section is one place to start but there are a number of ways of keeping colleagues included and up-to-date with your activities. Sharing the successes and the stories and demonstrating how your projects affect the public profile of the gallery can provide powerful advocacy for your work. Involving staff and giving them specific roles at relevant points of the project is an effective way of developing empathy, understanding and breaking down any anxieties about working with young people.

Ideas to help you raise the profile of your work both internally and externally:

- Produce a regular, concise and visual email diary for colleagues and partners
- Give presentations to the Board by or with young people
- Invite the chair of the Board or a local councillor to attend an activity
- Plan your project with a colleague, for example front of house manager, curator, marketing officer
- Write press releases and hold photo calls for internal and external press
- Produce concise and attractive written reports
- Invite colleagues and senior management to your celebration event
- Build staff training into new work – for yourself and colleagues
- Circulate case studies of young people's personal achievements
- Research opportunities for young people's artwork to be shown in other places and spaces, for example at the local library, at council offices, as greeting cards or invites, to illustrate leaflets, as entries into film or other cultural festivals
- Ask the young people to make a film about their experience

- Set up a MySpace page for the project
- Provide material for internal and external websites
- Invite a local youth magazine to write a feature about your project
- Create opportunities and support for young people, partners and staff to become ambassadors and champions of the project
- Present at a conference or seminar, with young people
- Organise a sharing event yourself
- Develop and disseminate resources for the gallery and youth sector

The envision projects in the east region also explored the viability of young people getting involved in the formal governance of galleries. The adults had reservations about young people being interested in attending regular committee meetings; the young people were also wary, but curious too:

❝I think it would be a good concept to see. I don't know whether I would want to go on it. I've not been in that situation before so I don't know my views and whether I would speak out. But if I did, if I really felt strongly about something, that would be great.❞

Young person, Enquire East: Learning for Empowerment, engage, 2007

Young People from Nottingham City Museums and Galleries projects, delivering a session at envision's Beyond Marketing seminar, 2005

organisations embracing youth-friendly practice

Sara Black, Director and Georgina Kennedy, Interaction Programmer, ProjectBase

- Young people inform and lead us in what we do, they are our creative future. Involving them in the work we do ensures that we take account of what they want and expect of working with contemporary artists. This continual dialogue enables me, as director, to consider innovative ways of working with artists and audiences.

- The best way to generate interest in youth-friendly practice with colleagues, directors and partners has been proven through advocacy and a multi-strand approach to disseminating the work we do. This includes formal approaches, such as written project reports, case studies and presentations and informal approaches such as advocacy and dissemination led by young people, for example documentary films (made, edited and directed by young people), youth-led websites (for our young people's programme) and support for young people, teachers and youth support workers to be cultural ambassadors in their own right. The practice of being 'youth-friendly' is in itself the best way to evidence the value of working with young people. The key to this has been making it visible to everyone we work with by involving them in the process, the outcomes and the impact.

- Over the last 18 months we have found the best way to generate interest from youth partners in the work we do has been through being flexible and sensitive to each organisation's individual needs, capacity and remit and working collaboratively with them to build peer-led initiatives with young people. We embed 'learning by doing' in all partnership projects and prepare project staff – from galleries and youth partners – to take part in this process. The three envision projects we have led have provided us with the opportunity to explore action research approaches to working with young people. From this we have recognised the value to all project staff from embedding time for shared reflection and review throughout the duration of projects. This approach has meant that staff from different organisations share skills, knowledge, experience and understanding, which provides a greater context for working in this way and greater opportunities for youth partners to recognise the cultural offer galleries and arts organisations provide to young people.

- Personally, the most significant thing I have learnt from working with young people is the potential for their ideas, observations and responses to impact on organisational strategy and forward planning. We have developed a large part of our Interaction Programme in response to ideas and enquiries made by people who have participated in our programmes. Through this process we have discovered how our programme can be forward thinking, responsive and innovative whilst embedding our audience at its heart.

> **"** Over the years we have developed a holistic approach, where education is truly integrated and all employees work in some way with project participants. Working with a gallery as a complete organisation is very different from working with an artist-in-residence or as an outreach project without a gallery link. This emphasis has been allowed by an active change in the culture of management of the organisation. For young people with turbulent lives, locating the gallery as a new place to come for support and encouragement increases their chances of accessing the help they need, both now and in the future. **"**

Rachel Tranter, Head of Arts, Richmond Borough Council at Orleans House Gallery

" When working with organisations it's often better to make small interventions well, rather than big sweeping changes, so take your time and don't think you can change the culture of an organisation overnight. I am often surprised that things that seems small and obvious to me can be life-changing or threatening to others. So, my advice is plant a few well chosen seeds and nurture them well. "

Clare Mitchell, Regional Youth Officer,
Government Office West Midlands

'Living Art', Metropole Gallery, 2007

Accrediting and valuing achievements

Accreditation

Offering accreditation to young people helps demonstrate the value of their achievement. For young people that have a negative relationship with formal education, it may provide a rare opportunity to accredit a learning experience.

The Arts Council's Arts Award scheme has proved beneficial for a broad range of young people involved in the envision programme and has been of particular value to young people with low self-confidence and little or no formal educational achievements. The award supports young people to develop as artists and arts leaders and is a nationally recognised qualification at three levels: Bronze, Silver and Gold, designed to be accessible to all young people. It can offer projects a framework and has encouraged young people to communicate their skills to others and to try new things.

Kings Lynn Arts Centre awarded three Bronze awards to young people working with them from the Pupil Referral Unit, as part of their accreditation they taught their new creative skills to children from a local primary school:

❝We taught the children to make paper out of scrap paper, shredded paper. And we're also doing felt making, which I'm in charge of. I volunteered to do it. I volunteered to lead the felt making, teach them how to do it. I was quite nervous at first. From there I got used to it and was comfortable.❞

Young person, Kings Lynn Arts Centre Links 4 project, Enquire East: Learning for Empowerment, engage, 2007

The Babylon Gallery in Ely researched how to deliver Arts Awards to a range of young people: gallery staff, sixth form students and members of Ely Young Carers group. Activities included workshops, exhibitions, manning stalls at career fairs and delivering sessions to other young people. Three Gold and two Bronze certificates were awarded.

See Resources for more ideas about accreditation options.

Celebration!

Building a celebration event into a project will provide an opportunity for the community, friends and family to value and share those achievements with you and the young people. Decide with staff and young people whether this will be a closed, invitation only event or an event open to the wider public.

An exhibition of young people's work can provide an important link between community and gallery, demonstrating young people have something positive to contribute to society, and that galleries are of relevance and importance to their local community.

Make sure you invite your manager and colleagues and get your partners to do the same – it's a perfect opportunity for a bit of advocacy and partnership building.

The event itself doesn't need to be very expensive, just drinks and nibbles – encourage the group to design an invitation that can be photocopied. They could invite friends, family, carers, partner organisations, key workers and gallery staff.

But the young people's artwork does need to be displayed as professionally as possible to give value, credence and status to the young people's achievements – try and get curators and technicians involved, meeting with you and the young people to discuss display ideas from the start.

If wall space is at a premium think creatively together about other places and spaces within the building (or outside it) that could be used. It doesn't necessarily need a three-month run; it could be a one night only event.

What next?

Once you've successfully run an activity, broken down some of the barriers, raised self-esteem, raised motivation and interest what happens next?

It's a good idea to have been thinking about the future potential of your project from the very start. How can you develop with what you've learnt and address the gaps in provision that emerge? This may change and expand as you get to know the young people and your partners and new or different opportunities arise.

Do some research and look into:

- In-house volunteering opportunities
- Youth partner opportunities
- Signposting to other local arts providers
- Fundraising with young people
- Further opportunities to work with project artists
- Setting up an advisory group to develop the programme further
- The need for a new post to develop this work further
- Continuing and developing the partnerships you've secured, organising a second version or a continuation of the project

If there is likely to be a large gap between one set of activity and the next try to sustain a dialogue with young people and keep them informed of developments through a newsletter, website, updates through partners, texts, events, invites to public events and volunteering opportunities.

'Game On' Qube Gallery, 2004

KickstART

After building enthusiasm and motivation Angela Blackwell, curator at the Thelma Hulbert Gallery in Honiton, supported the young people in putting their own bid into their local community fund and secured money to run the workshops and activities they wanted. They are currently working together to secure further funds to fund a youth panel co-ordinator post.

> **"** I have a real appetite to do more with young people and to make sure the youth panel continues. I am keen to see representatives for the youth panel on the exhibition selection committee and represented at other gallery management meetings. **"**
>
> *Angela Blackwell, Curator, Thelma Hulbert Gallery*

'KickstART', Thelma Hulbert Gallery, 2007

Over to you

We hope that through this book you have gained some practical insight and knowledge to stimulate and inspire your work with young people. Here are a few ideas of what you can do next:

Make contact with other arts and cultural organisations in your area and explore projects together

Do a presentation to the Board of your organisation about youth-friendly practice and get a commitment from them.

Find out who is responsible for writing the local development plan for Children's Services and how you could be written into it

Visit a local youth club, talk to the young people there and see where it takes you

Contact the Disabled Children's Service at your local authority and work with them to improve access at your gallery for disabled young people

Run training for artists on working with young people

Run a promotional campaign aimed at young people

Use it to develop your own policies and procedures

Use the www.teachernet.co.uk website to keep up to date with education policy and practice

Download and read Safe guarding Young People from the Arts Council website

IDEAS

Contact your local 14-19 education team and ask how you can get involved with the development of the Creative and Media Diploma

Partner up with a school or youth group and ask young people to design and update a specific youth section for your website

Become an engage member

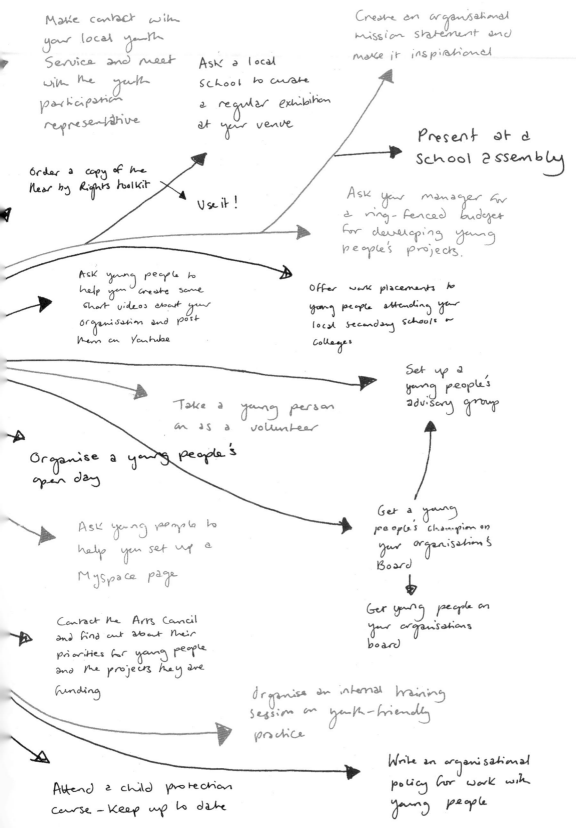

Make contact with your local youth Service and meet with the youth participation representative

Ask a local school to curate a regular exhibition at your venue

Create an organisational mission statement and make it inspirational

Present at a School assembly

Order a copy of the Near by Rights toolkit

Use it!

Ask your manager for a ring-fenced budget for developing young people's projects.

Ask young people to help you create some short videos about your organisation and post them on Youtube

Offer work placements to young people attending your local secondary schools or colleges

Take a young person on as a volunteer

Set up a young people's advisory group

Organise a young people's open day

Ask young people to help you set up a Myspace page

Get a young people's champion on your organisation's Board

Get young people on your organisations board

Contact the Arts Council and find out about their priorities for young people and the projects they are funding

Organise an internal training session on youth-friendly practice

Attend a child protection course – keep up to date

Write an organisational policy for work with young people

'Sample Arts', Ikon Gallery, 2004

Notes

Resources

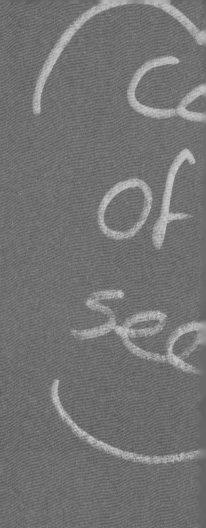

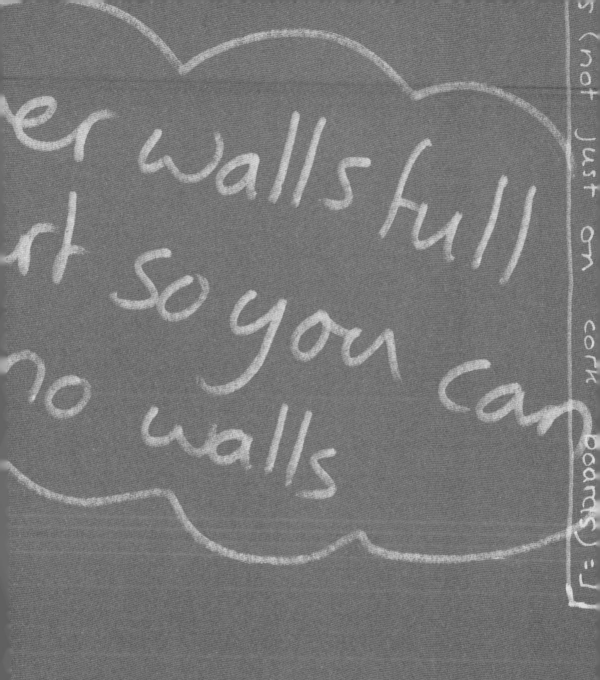

er walls full
rt so you can
no walls

(not just on cork boards) =]

Amber Walls

This section highlights key resources and places
where you can find other useful information to
keep yourself up-to-date.

The big ideas

Key issues, policies and initiatives

Aiming High for Young People is the government's 10-year strategy for positive activities to transform opportunities for young people in England, increasing their participation in high-quality leisure activities such as arts, sports and volunteering. The strategy outlines reforms based around three themes: empowerment, access and quality. For further details see www.dfes.gov.uk/public/ tenyearyouthstrategy and www.everychildmatters.gov.uk/ youthmatters/positiveactivities

Turning Point is Arts Council England's new strategy for the contemporary visual arts in England. Turning Point outlines the Arts Council's commitment to developing the role of contemporary visual arts over the next few years. One of the priorities is children and young people. Go to www.artscouncil.org.uk for more details.

Every Child Matters: Change for Children was introduced in 2004 and is the government policy at the heart of all work with young people from birth to 19 years old in England and Wales. If you are working with children and young people you need to know about it. Every Child Matters aims to ensure that all children and young people regardless of background or circumstances should have the support they need to achieve five outcomes: stay safe, be healthy, enjoy and achieve, make a positive contribution and achieve economic well-being. The policy demands that organisations working with children and young people work together in more effective ways through the develoment of Integrated Children's Services, managed by new Local Area Children's Trusts for each local authority. Under this new legislation Children's Trusts have new responsibilities, targets and funding providing potential partnership opportunties for galleries and museums working with children and young people. For more information see www.everychildmatters.gov.uk

Youth Matters builds on Every Child Matters, adopting the five outcomes for young people aged 13-19, encouraging opportuties for young people to have influence and choice over services provided for them. See the Youth Matters: Next Steps publication at www.everychildmatters.gov.uk/publications/ youth for more details.

The Cultural Offer/Find Your Talent sets out the government's commitment to providing a basic entitlement to cultural activity for all young people aged 0–19, with an emphasis on school age. It aims to ensure that all children and young people have the chance to participate in at least five hours of high quality culture a week in and out of school, involving: learning in and about culture – helping young people to develop as informed and reflective spectators, participants and creators, and learning through culture – using participation in culture to boost creativity, attainment and personal development.

14–19 Educational Reform aims to transform learning for 14-19 year olds. The reforms are designed to provide a more flexible range of learning routes suited to the diverse needs of learners and to the needs of employers, encouraging more young people to stay in post-16 learning. The Department of Education and Skills consulted with employers about new qualifications to recognise vocational achievement at ages 14–19. A specialised Creative and Media Diploma and apprenticeships schemes are being rolled out across the country, delivered by local consortia including schools, colleges and employers from autumn 2008. Employers from the cultural sector, including museums and galleries, are asked to support and develop these new initiatives.

Extended Schools will transform schools into community hubs, providing a range of services and activities within and beyond the school day for pupils, their families and the wider community. The Department for Children, Schools and Families (DCSF) is encouraging all schools to work with local partners to develop wider 'extended' services. Services will vary according to local needs but might include out-of-school-hours learning activities, health and social care, childcare, adult education and family learning, leisure activities and ICT access. Study support will be an important feature of extended schools, including after-school clubs creative projects, sports, games, mentoring and opportunities for volunteering and community activity. Schools developing extended services are required to develop a multi-agency approach through closer collaboration with schools, social services, healthcare professionals, police and other service providers who can support their extended service, which does of course include galleries. Go to www.teachernet.gov.uk/extendedschools or www.continyou.org.uk and www.standards.dfes.gov.uk/academies for more details.

'Sample Arts', Ikon Gallery, 2004

Specialist Schools Programme works in partnership with business sponsors with additional government funding to establish distinctive identities and raise standards through their chosen specialism, which includes the arts. Schools with arts specialism are encouraged to find new ways in which the arts can improve learning in other curriculum areas and can enable students to work with arts professionals and organisations to enjoy artistic experiences outside the classroom. If you are interested in working with specialist arts schools, your regional Arts Council office or your local Children's Services Education Team will be able to provide you with a list. Go to www.standards.dfes.gov.uk/specialistschools/ for more information and advice.

Artsmark is a national award scheme managed by Arts Council England, which recognises schools with a high level of provision in the arts. The award scheme is open to all schools in England: primary, secondary, special schools and pupil referral units, both maintained and independent. By gaining an Artsmark, a school shows its commitment to the wider development of young people and to raising the profile of the arts in the school and local community. Schools with or seeking Artsmark status are likely to be interested in what your gallery can offer them. Visit www.artscouncil.org.uk/artsmark/ to find out more.

Since 2005 local authorities across England have been working towards a contract called a **Local Area Agreement** (LAA) with central government. The aim of LAAs is to agree a set of standards, priorities and targets which meet both national government and local priorities. Each LAA has targets set by central government as well as some local ones. The Local Area Agreement is a plan delivered by all local government departments working with a wide range of local providers and communities. So if you work with local partners they are likely to be delivering work against LAA targets. The LAAs are currently organised into four main themes including a children and young people's theme. Contact your local authority or see their website for more details. Get a copy of the Local Area Agreement to see where it may be relevant to your work and find out who is leading on the children and young people's theme. If you're really interested you could visit www.idea.gov.uk as IDeA supports local government improvement and good practice and has produced information and resources about Local Area Agreements and other local government related issues.

Crossing the Line: Extending Young People's Access to Cultural Venues,
John Harland, Kay Kinder (eds), Calouste Gulbenkian Foundation and Arts Council England, 1999

This is a research publication exploring young people's relationship with cultural venues, presented through interviews, research findings and reflections.

Funky on Your Flyer, Richard Ings, Arts Council England, 2001
This book was commissioned as a result of Crossing the Line. Arts Council England commissioned a series of seminars across England using the research report findings to generate ideas and insights into how to increase young people's access to cultural venues.

Testing the Water: Young People and Galleries, Liverpool University Press and Tate Liverpool, 2000
A look at the pioneering Tate Liverpool programme for young people aged 14–25 years old. The publication includes a look at the wider context together with a collection of essays exploring how to create a workable strategy for sustainable youth programming.

engage Journal
A twice-yearly academic publication exploring current themes in the visual arts, galleries, access and education, published by engage and edited by Karen Raney. Each issue addresses a theme from the point of view of art practice, theory, education and curation. Some back copies are available from engage, others are available for reference only. There are specific issues on inclusion, interpretation, regeneration and research. www.engage.org/publications

Including Museums: Perspectives on Museums, Galleries and Social Inclusion, 2001
An interesting read if you have some spare time to reflect upon the issues and questions raised by the inclusion agenda for (art) museums. www.le.ac.uk/ms/bookshop/rcmg_publications.htm

The Arts and Social Exclusion, Helen Jermyn, Arts Council England, 2001
A publication about the debates around social exclusion and the arts. www.artscouncil.org.uk

'Living Art', Metropole Gallery, 2007

Getting started

Ideas and inspiration

envision, of course. See case studies at
www.en-vision.org.uk

Inspiring Learning in Galleries: Enquire about Learning in Galleries, engage, 2006
A fairly academic research report highlighting the findings from a national programme working with clusers of galleries across England to explore the particluar learning benefits of contemporary visual art to young people. Available from engage or you can download sections, such as enquire research findings and individual project reports from www.en-quire.org

Towards an Inspired Future: Creative Partnerships and Gallery Education,
engage 2006
A special engage and Creative Partnerships collaboration exploring the unique relationship between galleries and creative learning.
www.engage.org/publications

**Inspiration, Identity, Learning:
The Value of Museums,** Second Study,
DCMS/ DCFS, Research Centre for Museums and Galleries, 2007
An evaluation of the DCMS/DCFS national/regional partnership programme 2006–07. The study highlights lessons learnt through a programme bringing together over 50 regional museums with 12 national venues to develop local practice in order to strengthen local school and community partnerships. Useful case studies and information related to formal education, learning and social inclusion. Download a free copy or order a hard copy from www.le.ac.uk/ms/bookshop/rcmg_publications.htm

Renaissance in the Regions is a national programme working across the regions involving collaborations between museums, libraries and archive councils. Since 2002 government funding has enabled regional museums to raise their standards, develop beacons of good practice and deliver real results in support of education, learning, community development and economic regeneration, with a strong focus on benefitting young people. Renaissance has secured more funding from 2008 and will continue to develop programmes prioritising the following key themes; organisational development and change, collections, learning, widening participation (particularly amongst disabled and minority ethnic communities and areas of social and economic deprivation) and the cultural olympiad. www.mla.gov.uk/website/programmes/renaissance

UPSTART Youth Arts Directory,
Jonathan Keane, Artswork, 2005
A comprehensive directory of who's who in youth arts delivery, strategic development and funding opportunities in Great Britain.
www.artswork.org.uk

Planning

Culture and Learning: Creating Arts and Heritage Education Projects, Arts Council England and Heritage Lottery Fund, 2002
Although this was published in 2002 it is a comprehensive and practical guide to support the delivery of projects through conception, planning, delivery and evaluation. Download copies from www.teachernet.gov.uk/growingschools/resources or get a copy from enquire@hlf.org.uk or from www.artscouncil.org.uk

Targeting the Now Generation: A Case Study on Marketing the Arts to 15–19 year olds, St Catherine's College Oxford, 2001
This Arts Marketing Association publication is pretty old now but stands the test of time as a useful guide to marketing the arts to young people. www.info@a-m-a.co.uk

Working with specific groups

Artsplan guides. Artsplan is the professional development arm of Artswork, the national youth arts development agency. It produces over 20 specialist training courses and associated training guides or toolkits designed to meet the varying needs of professionals working with young people in the arts. Relevant titles include:

Using the Arts to Work With Young People at Risk, Virginia Haworth-Galt

Access all Areas: Disability and Youth Arts, Michelle Taylor

Developing Culturally Diverse Youth Arts Projects, Hatim Qureshi and Claire Wilkins

Using the Arts with Juvenile and Young Offenders, Vince Atwood

Using the Arts with Young Refugees and Asylum Seekers, Stella Barnes

Get Sorted: How to… Get Organised, Sort the Budget and Funding for Your Youth Arts Project, Ruth Jones

All published by Artswork, available for small fee from www.artswork.org.uk

The Art of Engagement: A Handbook for Using the Arts in Pupil Referral Units, Bob Adams with contributions from Shirley Brice Heath and Bianca Nunes, Janet Wood (ed), DARTS (Doncaster Community Arts), 2007

We love this book. A very practical guide to working in PRUs or with young people from PRUs based on extensive experience at DARTS. The contributions from Shirley and Bianca provide valuable theoretical insights into some of the practical situations and issues. Order from DARTS at www.thepoint.org.uk for a small fee.

Everything Stopped, Calouste Gulbenkian Foundation, 2007
A very moving fly-on-the-wall documentary showing the impact of the arts on young people who have been excluded from school. Copies of the DVD are available, free of charge, from Nick Randell Associates youth arts consultancy. To obtain a copy please email: dvd@nrassociates.co.uk

Creating Chances: Arts Interventions in Pupil Referral Units and Learning Support Units, Richard Ings, Calouste Gulbenkian Foundation, 2004
Explores the impact of recent creative projects in 12 centres around England which benefitted from First Time Projects funding available through the Gulbenkian Foundation and Arts Council England. This may be a useful source of ideas and case studies if you are new to PRUs and LSUs. Available from orders@centralbooks.com or 0845 458 9911

The Arts and Youth Justice: Arts and Young People at Risk of Offending,
Arts Council England and Youth Justice Board, 2006
Useful if you want to know about Arts Council and Youth Justice Board joint initiatives, such as the summer art schools and arts organisations working within the youth justice system. Downloadable at www.artscouncil.org.uk or to order from Marston Book Services via email at direct.orders@marston.co.uk

Doing it

Creating a Safe Environment

Keeping Arts Safe, Arts Council England, revised 2005

Arts Council guidance for individuals and arts organisations on child protection issues, as well as on devising policies and procedures to protect children, young people and vulnerable adults involved in arts activities. This free publication can be ordered from Marston Books via email at direct.orders@marston.co.uk or visit www.artscouncil.org.uk/publications for updated versions.

Stopcheck: A Step-by-Step Guide for Organisations to Safeguard Children, NSPCC, 2003 (updated 2007)

A guide for smaller organisations developing child protection policies and procedures. Send an A5 SAE with two first class stamps to NSPCC Publications, Weston House, 42 Curtain Road, London EC2A BNH or download at www.nspcc.org.uk

www.nspcc.org.uk

The National Society for the Prevention of Cruelty to Children (NSPCC) is a valuable site for information about child protection, duty of care policies, procedures and guidelines and publications.

www.crb.gov.uk

The Criminal Records Bureau (CRB) aims to help organisations in the public, private and voluntary sectors to work effectively and safely with children or other vulnerable members of society. The website will keep you up-to-date on current legislation around CRB checks.

Young vision

Supporting active participation and decision-making in galleries

Involving Children and Young People: An Introduction, National Youth Agency, 2007
This is a really useful handout taking you through the benefits of involving young people in your work. It includes basic values, traps and how to avoid them, and different ways in which you might support young people to shape and influence your work. Downloadable from *www.nya.org.uk*

Involving Children and Young People – Where to Find Out More, National Youth
Agency, 2005 This publication highlights a very useful top ten resources and reading around young people's participation, definition, models of participation and policy context. *www.nya.org.uk*

Hear by Right: Participation Standards Framework, National Youth Agency
Hear by Right is a tried and tested framework for organisations across the statutory and voluntary sectors to assess and improve their practice and policy on the active involvement of children and young people. It provides practical resources helping you to plan and assess your progress against three levels of practice: emerging, established and advanced. All the Hear by Right tools and resources are free to download. The website also includes case studies and an opportunity for you to promote your work online.
Go to www.nya.org.uk

www.en-vision.org.uk
Active participation was central to the envision programme and all envision case studies aimed to involved young people in shaping new practice, policy and organisational development. The website documents 32 diverse case studies involving young people at a range of levels.

What Do You Think? Artswork, 2007
The English National Youth Arts Network campaigns for creative youth consultation and participation. This is a practical toolkit supporting you to put into practice and campaign for creative youth consultation and participation. Available to download from www.enyan.co.uk

Participation Works is a national network
supporting youth participation and a website hub providing information, resources, news and networking on the involvement of young people in dialogue, decision-making and influence across a wide range of settings. For more details go to www.participationworks.org.uk

Creative resources for young people

The DCMS **Culture Online** website has links to some great resources and interactive sites including ArtisanCam a video and interactive resource for young people, which includes interviews from artists, curators and gallery technicians. Go to www.cultureonline.gov.uk

Access Arts is an online visual arts resource for learning and teaching. It includes a great interactive resource made with young people for young people called Teenage Creativity, and the Immersive Learning Space, a large site which explores the creative processes of different artists, dancers, architects, graphic designers etc. All this and more at www.accessart.org.uk

Wrapping up

Evaluation

Partnerships for Learning: A Guide to Evaluating Arts Education Projects,
Felicity Woolf, Arts Council England, revised and updated 2004

A very practical basic guide to evaluation that is widely used in the arts. Available free or download from Arts Council England at www.artscouncil.org.uk/publications

www.inspiringlearningforall.gov.uk
Inspiring Learning for All is a framework developed by the Museums, Libraries and Archives Council (MLA) designed to create a generic system to measure learning and improve provision in museums, libraries and archives.

Engaging Young People in Evaluation and Consultation, Big Lottery Fund Research Issue 10, research summary by Steve Browning and full report by Madeleine Swords, New Opportunities Fund, 2003
A very useful practical guide with tips on how to involve young people in accessible and creative evaluation activities.
Downloadable at www.biglotteryfund.org.uk

Capturing the Evidence: Tools and Processes for Recognising and Recording the Impact of Youth Work,
Hilary Comfort, Brian Merton and Malcolm Payne, Youth Affairs Unit, De Montfort University and Wendy Flint, The National Youth Agency, 2006
A practical toolkit to help facilitators working with young people to recognise and record the impact of youth work on participants. Offers a range of ideas and approaches particularly suited to youth work situations and partnerships. See www.nya.org.uk/publications. Price £13.50.

Youth Arts in Practice: A Guide to Evaluation, Linda Dixon and Nicola Aylward, National Institute of Adult Continuing Education, 2006
A practical toolkit designed to inspire and enable practitioners and managers delivering youth arts activities to evaluate projects. Suggests a range of creative and accessible evaluation approaches suiting different situations. The tools offered have been tested and adapted by five youth arts projects during a Partners in Innovation (PIN) action research project, and includes commentary from young people on their feelings about different evaluatiuon techniques. Available from www.niace.org.uk

Measuring Soft Outcomes and Distance Travelled: A Review of Current Practice,
Report Summary, DFES Research Report No 219, 2000
A research report on measuring 'soft' qualitative outcomes on a range of projects with socially excluded groups funded under the European Social fund. Available from www.employment-studies.co.uk/

engage 18 Research, Karen Raney (ed), engage, 2006
This issue of the engage journal looks at research methods used in the visual arts. A series of fairly academic papers look at different issues and ideas. Veronica Sekules presents the case for research in gallery education; Stephen Foster looks at the role of the gallery director and considers how academic research gets fed into a gallery context; Lewis Biggs looks at current thinking about fine art practice as research; Barbara Taylor writes on the enquire research programme and its interpretation of action research. Available from www.engage.org

Accreditation

The **Arts Award** supports young people aged 11–25 years old to develop as artists and arts leaders. It is a nationally recognised qualification at three levels: Bronze, Silver and Gold. Young people can work towards an award at an arts award centre, which can be any setting where arts activity happens, such as a gallery. Every centre must employ or be associated with at least one trained Arts Award adviser. The award has been developed to be accessible to all young people. It's designed to be flexible and to focus on an individual's personal interests and circumstances. There are no entry requirements, no time limits on completing the award and no hard rules on how work is presented. There are nine Arts Award agencies that promote the award and provide training and adviser support in each region. More information is available at www.artsaward.org.uk

ASDAN creates the opportunity for learners to achieve personal and social development through the achievement of ASDAN Awards and Qualifications, which focus on self-esteem, aspirations and individual contributions to local, national and global communities. The scheme offers a wide range of awards for young people of all abilities and recognises and rewards skills as 'personal challenges' are completed in areas such as, expressive arts, sports, healthy living, community involvement, work experience, and citizenship. The awards can be achieved in a variety of educational, training, employment, youth and community situations. Go to www.asdan.co.uk

The Assessment and Qualifications Alliance (AQA) is the largest of the three English exam boards and sets up and marks public exams such as GCSEs, A levels and other qualifications. There is also support for teachers and learners. They offer a broad range of academic and vocational qualifications including work based qualifications and entry level courses in art and design. See www.aqa.org.uk

The **National Open College Network (NOCN)** provides national qualifications and programmes in a wide range of subject areas (including the arts) and offers a local accreditation service, awarding credits in recognition of achievement. Each region will have a local Open College Network (OCN) provider that will give you advice and support in becoming a provider or linking up with other providers in your area. An OCN will work with your organisation to help make the courses flexible and accessible. Go to www.nocn.org.uk for more details.

National Vocational Qualifications (NVQs) are work related, competence based qualifications. They reflect the skills and knowledge needed to do a job effectively and are achieved through assessment and training. NVQs do not have to be completed in a specified amount of time and can be taken by full-time employees or by school and college students with a work placement or part-time job, there are no age limits and no special entry requirements. Go to www.qca.org.uk for further information.

The **Youth Achievement Awards** were initially established in the youth work sector as a means of recognising and accrediting young people's achievements and rewarding their involvement in decision-making. Recently, schools, colleges, national charities, youth offender institutions, youth offending teams, Connexions and training providers are finding them a valuable tool in motivating and engaging young people. There are different levels of award: Youth Challenges Awards aimed at young people aged 11–14 years, Bronze to Gold Youth Achievement Awards which are aimed at young people who are 14 plus, with the Platinum Young Leaders Awards being appropriate for young people of 16 plus. See www.ukyouth.org.uk for more details.

Online contacts

Young people

www.engage.org

engage is the international professional association supporting education and access to the visual arts through projects, research, advocacy, resource production and professional development programmes. If you're not already an engage member you need to join. The engage website provides information, resources, toolkits, case studies, research, professional and training opportunities and advice.

www.en-vision.org.uk

envision is engage's action research programme supporting the development of practice with young people aged 14–21 years old outside formal mainstream education, through action-research, training, seminars, networking, creation of resources and dissemination. The envision website hosts a valuable collection of case studies, resources, guidelines and useful information.

www.en-quire.org

enquire is engage's national research programme exploring, assessing and articulating the special learning benefits to young people of working with contemporary art and the gallery space. The enquire project is jointly funded by the Department for Culture, Media and Sport and the Department for Children, Schools and Families as part of the Strategic Commissioning Programme for Museum and Gallery Education, with support from the Foyle foundation. It has been developed in association with Arts Council England. enquire has supported regional clusters of galleries to work with researchers and local young people developing learning experiences (mostly but not exclusively with formal education) in galleries that have been thoroughly evaluated and reported on.

www.artswork.org.uk

Artswork is an independent national youth arts development agency which produces training, guidelines and resources, which also campaigns on behalf of the sector and manages ENYAN.

www.enyan.co.uk

English National Youth Arts Network (ENYAN) is a national network and professional resource designed to create connections throughout the diverse youth arts sector at national, regional and grass roots levels. ENYAN has regional advisory panels which seek to be the regional voice of youth arts and which occasionally organise regional activities. The panel is made up of people working in key youth/arts roles in each of the nine Arts Council England regions. ENYAN aims to raise the profile and support for youth arts in England. The ENYAN website is a fantastic free resource providing access to regularly updated news and policy developments advocacy campaigns, case studies, research, publications, professional development opportunities and access to local youth/arts networks.

www.artscouncil.org.uk

Arts Council England is the national development organisation for the arts in England. Check its website regularly for the latest developments in the arts and to source and keep updated on reports, publications and resources covering the arts and national policy and developments, funding, health, disability, diversity, education, access, audience development, evaluation and research as well as information on Arts Council strategic and grant aided projects.

www.creative-partnerships.com

Creative Partnerships is a programme that supports collaborations between formal education and creative and cultural providers which aim to increase the aspirations and achievements of young people. Creative Partnerships originally operated in areas of social deprivation but from 2008 has been rolled out to operate nationally. The Creative Partnerships website will be useful for developments in your area and also has a range of case studies and information related to the programme.

www.mla.gov.uk
The Museums, Libraries and Archives Council (MLA) is the national strategic body representing museums, archives and libraries. The website will tell you about national developments and recent policy, initiatives, campaigns, project reports, publications, contacts and opportunities within the sector as well as information on funding sources. Contact your regional office for information:

East
www.mlaeastofengland.org.uk

East Midlands
www.mlaeastmilands.org.uk

London
www.mlalondon.org.uk

North East
www.mlanortheast.org.uk

North West
www.mlanorthwest.org.uk

South East
www.mlasoutheast.org.uk

South West
www.mlasouthwest.org.uk

West Midlands
www.mlawestmidlands.org.uk

'KickstART', Thelma Hulbert Gallery, 2007

**www.mla.gov.uk/programmes/
renaissance**

This is the gateway to the national Renaissance in the Regions programme, which supports organisational and programme development in regional galleries and museums. The website has links for all the regional renaissance offices.

www.clmg.org.uk

The website for Campaign for Learning, a small organisation which campaigns for learning through projects, advocacy, campaigns and networking. The website has useful case study reports and publications.

www.voluntaryarts.org

The Voluntary Arts Network promotes participation to the arts across the UK. The website provides access to resources, news bulletins and information for the voluntary sector.

www.youthmusic.org.uk

Youth Music is the national organisation supporting youth music development. Provides advice and information, access to funding and information about strategic youth arts projects managed and developed by Youth Music, which are useful resources for anyone working on youth arts projects.

**www.teachernet.gov.uk/
teachingandlearning/
resourcematerials/museums/**

The teaching and learning area of the site has a specific page about learning in museums and galleries and carries information about current strategy, tips and links to lots of resources. New content is being added all the time, so return regularly for ideas.

Young people

www.nya.org.uk

The National Youth Agency website for policy, information, publications, guidelines and resources related to youth work nationally. It also produces good briefing papers on key issues or policy developments.

www.participationworks.org.uk

An online gateway for youth participation. Participation Works is a national network supporting youth participation. The website will also signpost you to your regional network, contacts and events.

www.youth-justiceboard.gov.uk

The Youth Justice Board oversees the youth justice system in England and Wales, working to address offending in young people under 18 years old. The website has information about the criminal justice system, strategic projects, resources and information about joint projects with Arts Council England, including Plus summer arts colleges and enrichment programmes delivered through the arts.

www.wearev.com

The website of V the national volunteering development agency. It's a lively and accessible website with a host of information and resources relevant to developing volunteering practice.

www.bbc.co.uk/blast

A young people's website providing access to opportunities, showcases and advice about careers in the arts. Blast is a BBC initiative to inspire creativity for 13–19 year olds in art, dance, writing, music and film. The website has information about BBC Blast activities in your area.

National policy and developments

www.everychildmatters.gov.uk
This website tells you everything you need to know about the delivery of Every Child Matters and related education and youth strategies. It includes lots of useful information sheets that summarise new developments.

www.dcfs.gov.uk
The Department for Children, Families and Schools (DCFS) website houses information and contacts related to work with young people, families and education.

www.culture.gov.uk
The Department for Culture, Media and Sport (DCMS) website houses developments, national policy, statistics and sector research related to culture.

www.communities.gov.uk
The Department for Communities and Local Government (DCLG) website houses information relevant to communities and local government, including Local Area Agreements.

Education

www.aliss.org.uk
Artists Learning and Information Support Service (ALISS) is a West Midlands based network with a range of education information and resources. Although regionally based, the information is relevant nationally.

www.prus.org.uk
The National Organisation for Pupil Referral Units website houses useful information about working in PRUs and includes arts case studies, professional development events, and downloadable reports and publications.

www.capeuk.org.uk
Creative Arts Partnerships in Education (CAPE UK) specialises in creativity through research based project work, consultancy and professional development. It works with schools in the Leeds and Manchester areas to explore new ways of approaching the curriculum but also works in informal contexts targeting young people experiencing exclusion. A useful website with resources about its own and related work.

'Every Drawing Matters', Orleans House Gallery, photo by Haken Yazici

envision projects
2002–2008

Phase one

Qube Gallery, Oswestry
MediaMaker
Partners: Kingswell Centre (Pupil Referral Unit),
Craftspace Touring, ShYAN (Shropshire Youth
Arts Partnership and ALISS (Artists Learning,
Information and Support Service)

The Royal Pump Rooms, Leamington Spa
Connect 4
Partners: WYAN (Warwickshire Youth Arts
Network)

Ikon Gallery, Birmingham
Sample Arts
Partners: BAYC (Birmingham Association
of Youth Clubs)

Manchester Art Gallery
Creative Consultants

Zion Arts, Hulme, Manchester
Young Participants and Curators

Cornerhouse, Manchester
LiveWire

Nottingham Castle Museum and Art Gallery
Wordz Out

Angel Row Gallery, Nottingham
Way in Way Out
Partners: Nottingham City Youth Service
and the APT youth arts project at City Arts

Phase two

NWDAF (North West Disability Arts Forum),
Liverpool
Inside Out
Partners: Tate Liverpool

198 Gallery, Brixton
Excelerate

Bow Arts Trust, Bow
Our Vision, Our East End
Partners: Central Foundation School for
Girls and Bow School

Orleans House Gallery, Richmond
Every Drawing Matters
Partners: Richmond Children's Services

List of evision projects

ProjectBase, Penzance
Art Ambassadors
Partners: Cornwall Youth Service, Treviglas School, Redruth School, Cornwall College, Cambourne, Tate St Ives and Newlyn Gallery

Spacex Exeter
X-Panel (Handover)
Partners: The Siblings Project (working with the younger siblings of offenders)

Q Arts, Derby
Sparks
Partners: local schools

Hub: National Centre for Craft and Design, Sleaford, Lincolnshire
My Space: Your Space
Partners: ArtsNK

Phase three

Milton Keynes Gallery
Consultation Workshops
Partners: Milton Keynes Gallery Young People's Steering Committee

Fabrica, Brighton
Straight Talking
Partners: Brighton & Hove City Council Youth Offending Team

Metropole Galleries, Folkestone, Kent
Living Art
Partners: Kent County Council Attendance and Behaviour Service

Artsway, Hampshire
Generator
Partners: Wessex Youth Offending Team and Isle of Wight Youth Options

Thelma Hulbert Gallery, Honiton, Devon
KickstART
Partners: The Ivy (youth volunteering organisation)

Study Gallery, Poole
My Art Space Too
Partners: Corfe Hill School

ProjectBase, Penzance
Art Ambassadors II
Partners: Tate St Ives, Cornwall, Detached Youth Service – Kerrier District, Newlyn Gallery, Equality & Diversity Services (Children's Services Authority Cornwall), Poltair School, St Austell

Phase four

Scarborough Art Gallery
Young Vision
Partners: Youth Arts Training Scheme, Foundation Housing and Community Education Service

Site Gallery, Sheffield
Envision Project
Partners: Shift Media (E2E providers) and Cube youth magazine

Ferens Art Gallery, Hull
Find Out and Feed In
Partners: Kingston Upon Hull Youth Offending Team and Fountain House Pupil Referral Unit

Babylon Gallery, Ely
Arts Award Delivery Project
Partners: local sixth form students and Ely Young Carers

Kings Lynn Arts Centre
Links 4
Partners: Rosebury Centre Pupil Referral Unit

Outpost, Norwich
NR5 into Outpost
Partners: NR5 alternative education centre

NR5, Norwich
Future Education into the Sainsbury Centre for Visual Arts Project
Partners: Sainsbury Centre for Visual Arts, Norwich

Sainsbury Centre for Visual Arts, Norwich
Enquire Project